Just One More Mile

MOLLY POLLACK

authorHOUSE®

AuthorHouse™
1663 Liberty Drive
Bloomington, IN 47403
www.authorhouse.com
Phone: 1-800-839-8640

First published by AuthorHouse   8/18/2010

ISBN: 978-1-4520-5575-6 (e)
ISBN: 978-1-4520-5574-9 (sc)

Library of Congress Control Number: 2010911889

Printed in the United States of America

This book is printed on acid-free paper.

CONTENTS

PROLOGUE

My name is Molly Sherman. My life style was so different from yours; you may find it hard to believe. Today you are so sheltered. A Jewish child in Russia 100 years ago was forced to grow up very quickly...

OUR LIFE IN RUSSIA

As was customary in those days, when my father was ten years old, his mother informed him that he was engaged to be married.

The marriage had been arranged years before either my mother or father were born, and right after his Bar Mitzvah, 13 year old Avram married 12 year old Raizll. For a while the young couple lived with my father's mother. He was already earning money as a cantor, but gave it all to his mother, who just gave the couple what they needed for expenses.

As was traditional, for her entrance into married womanhood, my mother had had all her hair shaved off, and put on a wig.

My father became a popular cantor, and toured all over Russia and beyond to China, Irkutsk, Japan and Turkey.

My mother was a quiet woman who never raised her voice to anyone and had the patience of an angel. She had twelve children, six of whom lived to adulthood.

I was the fifth of six children I lived with my parents, two sisters, and a brother in a small house among other Jews in the village of Meropol. My two older brothers were married and lived in the United States.

Our house was crowded with beds and there was very little privacy. My two older sisters and I shared my bed. The bed boards that served as a spring, often fell through, and we would find ourselves on the floor. My mother would hear us and got up to fix the bed boards in again. "Try not to move too much," she would say before she went back to bed.

That winter was dark and sad. The weather was cold and so windy that snowdrifts came up higher than the windows. Our windows were always doubled in the winter and sealed with strips of paper, glued over the cracks and hinges.

Our stack of wood was getting alarmingly low. We had no choice but gather some broken branches from the forest almost a mile away. My two older sisters would bundle up pulling our home made sled downhill towards the forest.

The snowy branches they brought back were damp and hard to burn. My father would blow and blow on the fire, but to no avail. Then there was no other choice but to pour some of the precious kerosene over the smoky branches to get the fire going. I was bitterly cold and hungry, but I dared not complain.

I would have eaten anything to satisfy my hunger. A carrot, a potato, or even watery soup would have helped. My mother continuously was search for food. She would rise in the coldest weather real early and visit the Ukrainian farmers to buy something. Sometimes she was lucky and managed to bring something and sometimes she would return empty-handed.

After the synagogue burned down my mother's hands were never still. Without the synagogue, it was impossible for my father to earn a living as a cantor. So now the whole burden of supporting our large family fell on her.

To earn money, my mother would mend rubber overshoes for the farmers and knit heavy woolen gloves for the soldiers. At meals she would always say she wasn't hungry so that we would have some more to eat.

I noticed that my mother didn't bake as often as she used to. I remember opening the bread cabinet where we kept the bread. I found it empty. There wasn't even a crumb.

At dinner my mother set down one bowl of soup on the table and we began to spoon from it. She pretended that she wasn't hungry after two spoons of soup. There was no meat and only a few potatoes and a small piece of bread for each of us.

The shortage of food increased and the stores became more and more empty of the necessary items. The market had almost nothing left to sell and the feeling of hunger swept across our town.

The second winter of the war things became from bad to worse. Potatoes were cooked with the jackets on so there won't be any bit of potato wasted.

My mother worked harder than ever. But the farmers gave her very little food now as they hardly had enough for themselves.

An egg was now a luxury in our household. My mother would always add a little water so it could be portioned out. The shelves from our pantry became bare. There used to always be jelly, chicken fat, sugar, tea, flour, and salt, now there was hardly any left and we couldn't replace them.

We had been issued ration books for use at the state store only. There were always long lines in front of the store, but the food was quickly sold and many people were turned away. After staying in line in the cold for many hours my mother would return home empty handed.

Flour and sugar were fast disappearing from our household. Now a dry pear was a substitute for sugar, a potato for bread. We all spooned from the same soup bowl. My portion of meat would be the width of a noodle.

Women were assigned to the soldiers' kitchen to peel potatoes and, in return, they were permitted to keep the potato peels. My sisters would bring home the potato peels from the soldiers kitchen and my mother would wash them and make a soup out of them adding beans, barley, and a carrot if she had any.

One day I took a little knife and followed my sisters to the soldiers' kitchen. At the door a Russian soldier stopped me. "This is not for little girls," he said.

"I'm seven years old and I can peel really well." I replied with pride. The soldier gave me a potato as a test. I was extra careful and peeled the potato in long curls. The soldier was impressed. I was soon sitting on the floor with the rest of the women peeling potatoes. When we were finished I took my share of the potato peels home.

One day I put a few little potatoes in the sack when no one was looking. I was nervous as I picked up my sack, but the soldiers didn't pay attention to me.

When I got home my mother was in the kitchen, her face was smudged with soot from the flying cinders as she blew on damp pieces of wood to make the fire going.

"Mama, mama! Look what I got," I cried with excitement as I spilled the potato peels on the table and took out the three little potatoes.

I thought I would see a smile on her face, but instead she looked at me fearfully. "Malke, I know that you're hungry, but it's still stealing. Besides, if you get caught we would all be in trouble. Please don't do that again."

I remember that water was very precious. There was no such thing as a running water tap. Water had to be carried from the community well a block away.

There was no well pump, so water had to be drawn up by hand. That was quite a trick. We had to lower the pail on a long rope to exactly the right distance above the surface of the water, then, with a snap of the wrist, flip the pail over and sink it. Carefully we would haul up the brimming pail without spilling a drop, untie the rope, and carry our drinking, cooking, and washing water home.

Without even a washboard to help, the laundry chores never ended. Back and forth, back and forth to the well, it took my mother all week to wash and dry. Like the other women, she had to do everything by hand. She had to do all of the baking, sewing, cooking, preserving, and even making her own goose feather pillows and lace curtains.

I would tag along every time my mother went to the market, but I was only interested in dolls that were displayed on tables. The dolls looked strangely alive as if they were breathing. I stood there fascinated but I didn't dare ask my mother to buy me one. I never had the luxury of choosing between several dolls. I had none at all.

Finally, my mother made me a cloth doll. It satisfied me for a while, but as I grew older, my desire for a real doll got stronger. Eventually it seemed as if nothing else mattered.

At last, when I had the measles, my wish came true. A doll was found at a bargain price. One of its pinkies was chipped, and its red and blue dress was soiled but I didn't care. To me it was the most beautiful doll on earth, and my eyes never left its rouged porcelain cheeks.

I didn't have many toys, but what I did have was an overactive imagination. I loved to make up stories, which the other kids listened to with their eyes wide open, craving more. I even staged little plays in our woodshed.

My parents were terrified that their child, their little girl, was acting like a profesional in a show with teen-agers. I remember writing something in my notebook, a little story about an orphan girl getting lost in the woods where she was saved by an angel. I was the star and the building, which was rented for the show, was overflowing with people.

But nice children didn't become actors then. My parents looked down on such things. There was no training; no encouragement and my parents forbade me to act ever again. Although I had great desire to act again and it was a great disappointment to my eight-year-old mind.

Musicians were never respected for their talent. They were looked down upon and were regarded as odd characters. They played by ear because there weren't any music schools or teachers. The group of musicians was called klezmer. They were hired to play at weddings. They would play all kinds of traditional Jewish songs never looking at a note, but they seemed pretty good. This was how they earned a living.

I had a talent for dancing, and used to imagine everybody paying a lot of rubles to watch me.

Once we were invited to a wedding, and my oldest sister, Goldie, decided to make me a dress. Mama supervised the cutting out, and Goldie basted the dress with white cotton, but time ran out. The ceremony was ready to begin. If we were going to get to the wedding on time, I had to go in the basted dress. My brother and I danced the Russian Waltz and we were a hit, but my mother was a nervous wreck worrying that my basted dress would come apart. However it never did.

A month before Yom Kippur, as was the custom, a chicken was bought for every member of the family. My chicken was little with yellow feathers and I became attached to it. Every single morning I would walk into the woodshed where the chickens were and feed my little chicken grain from a pan and watch it pick the grain. I watched it grow bigger and fatter.

My mother would show them off to her neighbors with great pride. Days passed into weeks. It was now time for our fowl to be slaughtered by the shochet.

I carried my little chicken to the shochet slaughterhouse. Its legs were bound with strings. My two older sisters and brother carried their own chickens.

The shochet, a thin man with earlocks and a tattered gray beard on his head rested a yarmulke. With his sleeves rolled up, his coat tails tucked into his trousers, he was now ready for action.

A woman pushed forward with her rooster. I watched the shochet grab the chicken and turning it's head with his left hand to pluck the fine feathers of it's neck while he held the knife between his teeth. When he removed some of the feathers from it's neck he cut it's neck with one quick slash of the knife then dropped the fowl to the floor where it continued to struggle for a few minutes before it collapsed.

I stood there watching that murder for a few minutes clutching my little chicken to my chest, which was about to get the same fate. I turned and ran away clutching my chicken. At home I ran up the ladder to our attic and hid the chicken in a barrel.

My mother looked everywhere for me and couldn't find me. Finally, my sister found me and took my little chicken away. My eyes in tears I ran into the house.

"Malke," my mother explained. "We must kill some of the animals so we can eat and be strong."

"But we can eat bread, Mama."

"We cannot only live on bread alone. When you'll get older you'll understand." Somehow I eventually got over it.

Yom Kippur was the holiest day of the year. It is a day of atonement that calls for the fasting by both sexes who had reached the age of thirteen. I watched those sad faces of the women who sat on the balcony in the synagogue separated from the men, as was custom. The cantor garbed in white stood before the ark on the reader's platform. He sang ancient prayers to traditional melodies accompanied by his choir.

The women wept as they prayed. The glimmer of the candles in brass chandeliers was bowed as if they, too, were in prayer. My mother's face showed the weariness of worry as she bowed in prayer. They all prayed for survival of the war.

Again and again power of government changed hands. Men were arrested were never brought to trial. They simply disappeared. I could not imagine any other way for people to live except for being cold and hungry. I had grown older and wiser during all the sufferings of the war, although I was still no more then eight years old.

"You're so young, you shouldn't know what sadness is," my mother said one day.

The wood we bought for the winter was shrinking fast as the winter was the coldest we had ever experienced. Adding to our problems I had no shoes. I had outgrown them, but there was no money for new ones. So my mother unraveled a potato sack and used the strings to make me a pair of slippers but I couldn't walk outside with them so I stayed mostly in bed.

Despite the hard times we drew our strength from my fathers humor. He would often joke about my homemade slippers, and about the tea that was made from rainwater. "It tastes like my mothers cooking," he would joke.

He would also give the neighbors moral support. "Tomorrow is another day and it will get better," he would say, "Have faith in God." He would entertain them with a story or two and before they knew they were laughing, temporarily forgetting their problems. They found a friend in my father and ask his advice, which he readily gave them with confidence.

My father's historic stories had a special appeal to me. He made them sound so vivid, so alive as if I was right there when it happened.

My father's sense of humor was wholehearted and mostly at his own expense. Over a glass of tea, he would be so funny that our friends would laugh at times to coughing fits. He had this tremendous talent, but I don't think he realized it.

In a moment of peace in the winter evenings neighbors from close by would ever so often drop in for a glass of tea. My father's humor sent our visitors into peels of laughter, sometimes to coughing fits. Despite the war, cold and hunger, my father always gave us all a lift by his jokes, and humor.

THE WAR

I had my first personal experience with war when nineteen horsemen led our town's chief of police out to be executed. He was still in his nightclothes and barefooted. I remember it was winter, and the streets were icy. I was standing in a small gathering of our townspeople. A peasant woman made the sign of the cross. I could hear the man's wife screaming in the distance. The sound pierced me, and a shiver went through my body. I heard those screams when I played, ate or slept.

One day I heard the news that tsar Nicholas had been dethroned. His own soldiers who were supposed to protect him had backed the revolutionaries.

Then next day, everything changed. I became aware that young fellows from our neighborhood were in uniforms. Mothers wept as they bid farewell to their sons who were leaving for war.

The next morning I awoke to the clatter of horses hoofs on our cobblestone streets and the harsh shout of military commands. I looked out the window and saw countless Russian soldiers, rifles flung over their shoulders, followed by horse drawn wagons and horsemen. Our little town was soon overrun with them.

The secret police and militia often raided Jewish homes searching … always searching.

One night, a nightmare woke me up in the middle of the night. I heard shouting, running feet, curses and then shots. It wasn't a bad dream, it was real. I heard a loud pounding on our door. "Open up!" a gruff voice shouted. My mother hastily threw some clothes on and opened the door. Several men in uniform carrying lanterns stormed into our house. Pushing my mother out of the way they began to search. They searched everywhere, in our rooms and even under beds. Then they ran into our woodshed running up the ladder to the attic, and then running back down again. Satisfied, they finally left.

Things kept happening all the time. Men who were suspected of membership of the underground were arrested and executed in the forest. The forest, which was once a beautiful place to visit, became a place for executions. The bells of the church boomed almost constantly for the dead.

One morning, I awoke to the roar of a bomb explosion. The whole house shook. Chunks of plaster from the wall by my bed fell on me, and I scrambled onto the floor. Then the whole wall came crashing down, covering my bed with debris.

Worse yet, our brick oven caved in. Now Mama had no way of cooking.

Even so, we had a lot to be thankful for. We had miraculously escaped with no personal injury and our home still standing, while many people in our town had been killed or left homeless.

The lack of our oven was a big problem, however. Neighbors tried to help by letting my mother use their ovens. My Uncle Pinnie promised to rebuild ours if he could just get some bricks.

I loved Uncle Pinnie and his booming laugh. He was like a talking newspaper. He knew everybody and everything about everybody, and what he didn't know, he made up. When he got excited about something, he coughed a lot, interrupting himself when he was telling the news. I remember his visiting at teatime in better days. Holding a cube of sugar between his teeth, he would drink glass after glass of tea from the steaming samovar.

I decided I would get the bricks for Uncle Pinnie to rebuild our oven. One day I searched in the burned-out homes nearby, but they had all been wooden structures. Then, near the school, I spied a demolished brick building. I felt as if I'd discovered the biggest treasure in the world.

The bricks were very heavy, so I could only carry one at a time. Day after day on my way home from school I picked up another brick. Brick by brick, Uncle Pinnie rebuilt the oven.

When the oven was almost finished, I was searching the ruins for another brick, when I suddenly heard voices. Startled, I looked around, and found myself staring at several peasant boys about my own age. They looked mean.

"Hey'" one of them yelled to another. "There's that Jew girl who's been stealing all your father's bricks. Let's get her!"

I dropped the brick and ran like a rabbit. A stone struck the back of my head as I ran, then another my shoulder, but I got away relatively unharmed.

I didn't dare go back for more bricks again, but by this time, the oven was so close to being repaired, that Uncle Pinnie was able to complete the job with some stones.

Then toward spring the fighting finally stopped. Everybody began to talk all at once.

"Thank God, Thank God, the war is over," they would say. But the post war wasn't much better. We still couldn't get food, but at least there was no more booming of bombs. We slept now in peace.

The year that followed the Russian Revolution brought change after change. There were always new leaders and new dictators. Speakers, their chests decorated with all kinds of ribbons, and medals, their sleeves with emblems garbed in their uniforms, often stood on platforms and spoke in front of a crowd with great passion and conviction promising all kinds of blessings.

"Hurrah! Hurrah! Hurrah!" shouted the crowd in one thunderous voice into a defining roar tossing their caps in agreement. At other times they paraded with banners and song.

Our little town was now under the new Bolshevik rule. Waves of arrests were aimed at political groups who had contact with the old Russian government. The sweep was made by the secret police. Intellectuals, Barons, teachers, the commissar, and many others were led away and never heard from again. Meropol was now alive at night with the rapping on doors and the dragging of men from their homes, and people scurrying to find hiding places. The intruders were tall and husky carrying rifles over their shoulders.

The new regime was turning schoolboys into spies. They were brainwashed and bribed by the Bolsheviks. "Report to us everything you see or hear. As a good citizen of Russia, you must be loyal and spy on your friends, relatives, and even on your own father and mother. If you do well you'll be promoted to a high rank and be rewarded with some pocket money."

People began to distrust each other especially when young boys were near by listening. Parents were now afraid of their own children.

The government took the word of the informer without checking. You were in trouble if you had a personal enemy. Men were arrested everywhere, both outside their homes and inside. No one heard from them again.

No one suspected the young boy named Sasha was a spy for the Bolsheviks. He was twelve years old and lived with his parents and sister next door to us. Sasha was a quiet boy with a shy manner, but a loner. He had very few friends. We were all stunned when he was accusing his own father of being against the new government. Six people were arrested on Sasha's say so and executed without a trial. He then began to keep watch on his own father, Misha. His life was now at stake. Misha had no choice but go into hiding from his own son.

From the changing governments, my parents' savings vanished very quickly. Soon there were bomb explosions and fires, and then almost no food to be found, until a dry crust became a luxury. My mother would stand in line for hours in freezing weather for only half a pound of bread, and even then, sometimes had to come home empty-handed.

Life became uncertain. We never knew what to expect. In the middle of the night there was always rapping on our door by Bolsheviks or Germans searching for someone. Footsteps were always running up the ladder in our woodshed checking for people in hiding. Dogs were used to sniff them out.

One day Uncle Pinnie rushed in excitedly to warn us that the Cossacks were coming. We froze with fear, for the Jewish people knew that the Cossacks were known for their atrocities.

Then my mother took charge. "Get to bed and play sick," she commanded my sister Goldie. "You get behind the trunk and hide," she said to my other sister Lily. Then she gathered up every medicine bottle she could find and put them on the table next to the bed. She opened some of the bottles, and spilled out medicine, until the whole room smelled of it. Then she covered Lily in her hiding place with pillows.

Soon there came a rapping on the door. My mother quickly commanded my younger brother and I to hide underneath the bed. My father hurried up the ladder into the attic. Then Mother threw open the door. Three Cossacks, sabers at their sides and rifles over their shoulders, thrust themselves inside. From where I was hiding under the bed, all I could see was their spurred boots.

I heard one of them ask my mother what was wrong with my sister.

"Scarlet fever," Mother answered.

"Scarlet fever'" he repeated with a curse. The three soldiers almost fell over each other as they ran out.

Mother quickly told Goldie to write a sign reading "Scarlet Fever" in Russian. It hung outside our house, and the rest of the Cossacks passed us by.

In time the troops began to leave our town. We could again sleep nights without being awakened by scream and shots. The sounds of the people rejoicing to the music of the Polka filled the air.

PAVA

I was very small when my mother bought a cow. She was very pretty with a healthy brown coat and there was a white spot right between her eyes. We named her Pava.

My mother with a twig in her hair would take Pava to the pasture every single morning, but return home by herself before sundown. A bucket of water was always waiting for Pava in our alley where she would drink with great gulps and then stand with dripping nostrils over the empty pail and moo.

On a shelf in the barn was the milking pail. My mother picked up the pail, put it underneath the cow and sat down on a small stool and expertly began to milk Pava. Milk began to squirt and boom into the pail, which sounded like a drum. When she was finished milking her, my mother gave us all a glass of milk. The rest of the milk went into two pitchers.

One day, our cow gave birth to a baby calf. It was so beautiful lying on the straw. It also had a white spot between its eyes just like its mother.

I watched Pava hover over the calf, breathing on it, nudge it gently with her nose, and make soothing sounds to it until it stood up on its spindly legs and looked for it's mother's udder. When the calf got bigger and was able to drink milk from a bucket and eat grass, my mother sold it.

One day Pava didn't return home at her usual time before sundown so my mother went to look for her in the meadow where she was grazing. Pava was lying down and couldn't get up because she had a broken leg. My mother had no choice, but to sell her to a butcher who would put our cow out of her misery.

The next morning four men went to the meadow and piled our cow into a horse-drawn wagon and brought her to our woodshed.

There she was harnessed up by a thick rope which suspended her in mid-air. All the time she bellowed so loud that it gave me goose bumps. She strained at the ropes and kept bellowing as if she was begging for her life.

"Mama, mama," I cried and tugged at her sleeve. "Don't let them hurt Pava!" Tears were running down my face.

"Take your little girl out of here!" one of the man shouted, sharpening his knives at the same time.

"No," I screamed, "Leave my Pava alone!" But it fell on deaf ears. My mother took my hand and gently took me outside the woodshed, but I could still hear the cow bellowing almost like a human being.

Then suddenly, all was quiet. No more sounds came from our woodshed. It was all over my beloved Pava was slaughtered by those men, and cut into sections of meat, ready for the housewives to buy and cook.

It was a horrible experience for my five-year-old mind. I often had nightmares about our cow and would wake up crying. "We'll buy another cow," my mother promised.

"No, mama, no, " I cried. It took almost a year before the memory of our cow began to fade. It was an experience I can never forget.

MY EDUCATION IN THE RUSSIAN SCHOOL 1917

I was still very little when I began to attend the cheider. It was a one room in the rebe's house where it always smelled of food. In cheider, the children would sit on benches around the long table, which stood in the middle of the room.

After awhile I went to another Jewish school where I learned how to read and write in Yiddish. The school was only one room in the teacher's house. I was a good student, but I wasn't satisfied with Hebrew and Yiddish alone, 1 wanted to learn how to read and write in Russian.

I would often watch the gentile children walk home from school carrying their books chatting and laughing happily. How I would envy them. I wasn't like the other children in the neighborhood. While they played with dolls, I had to use my imagination. I was curious about everything and I would shower my mother with all kinds of questions like, "where do the butterflies come from" or "what makes the bird fly".

"When you get older you'll find out," she would always say.

I was never lavished with attention or pampered with toys. Toys to my mother were a waste of money. It never crossed my mind that children my age in another country had dolls to play with and lot's of nice dresses I thought little girls suppose to wear cast off clothes from their older sisters and walk barefoot in the summer to save shoes.

I had an overactive imagination. The run down house with the twisted old trees suddenly became a palace with a big orchard; the empty lot across the way became a beautiful rose garden.

I also had a talent telling stories to the children of the neighborhood. I would make up tales about kings, queens, devils, and even ghosts, and the children would all sit around me listening with their mouths open begging for more.

I would write all of my stories down on paper. I wrote them in Yiddish, but I would have liked to be able to write some of them in Russian.

"Mama, can you buy me a Russian book," I begged.

"What good would that book do you if you can't read Russian? I'll hire Ruhel to teach you. I have heard that she can read and write very well in Russian."

"You promise?" I asked my mother happily.

"Yes, I promise", she replied smiling.

Ruhel was a fifteen-year-old girl with two long braids who was an avid reader. My mother hired her for a few silver coins a week. I soon learned what she knew, and I still wanted to learn more. I drove her crazy with questions. Finally she told my mother that she couldn't teach me any more.

"Mama, why can't I go to the Russian school?" I kept pestering my mother, which drove her up a wall. I didn't understand that Jewish children were denied a Russian education. My mother had been there earlier with her older children and was rejected. My mother knew that it was a waste of time, but to please me she decided to try again.

It was a cold September day and I clutched my mother's hand with excitement. We were headed towards the Russian elementary school. The school was over a mile away, but I didn't mind. We passed the church, the bridge, and were now on the outskirts of the town. We passed the gentile section, which was very dangerous. Dogs or even young children could have attacked us.

I had never been in this section before. Their huts were different from ours and there were so many trees that, although they were losing their leaves, still looked pretty. In the Jewish neighborhood there were hardly any trees or gardens except for the empty lot across the street where wild grass grew.

Snowflakes were coming down now one by one, but my mother ignored them. A horseman passed us by without giving us a second glance. We finally turned into a side road and I saw an old one story building with lots of windows and a small porch. It was early morning and students were still going into the building. They turned their heads and stared at my mother and me.

My mother hesitated for a moment, and then she slowly opened the heavy wooden door and walked in holding me by the hand. We found ourselves in a dark gloomy corridor. It was still early as the students were still coming in and stared at us quizzically as they walked into their classroom. I had never seen a Russian school before. My mother asked one of the students where the teacher was.

"He isn't here yet," she replied. We stood there in the darkened hall waiting. Finally a large man appeared. He was tall with a long, drooping mustache that reached his chin. I could see that he was surprised to see us there.

"Dobra Utra," my mother greeted him in Russian.

"Dobra Utra," he replied with his loud booming voice. "What can I do for you?" He asked with a stern face.

"I would like to enroll my little girl in your school." She beamed with pride as she took out some of work that I have done with the Jewish girl who had taught me. "This is her work. She is a very good student and ..."

"I'm sorry, this school is for gentile children only."

"Why?" my mother asked. "Doesn't a Jewish child have a right to learn?"

"It's not all up to me. You see ..."

"Mr. Gorky, I've been here so many times before with my older children and have been denied. Please don't disappoint this child she is so anxious to attend your school that she even talks in her sleep about it."

He stood up and looked out the window. "Let me think for a day or two I'll let you know what I can do for you"

But my mother didn't budge. "No, please, make up your mind now. I'll pay you whatever you ask."

I could see that he was thinking but couldn't make up his mind. He kept staring at me and at my mother and I saw a flicker of sympathy in his eyes.

"All right, I'll make an exception, but it will cost you five rubles a month."

My mother caught her breath. Five rubles was a lot of money, and she knew that we couldn't afford it, but she didn't dare to bargain. She took out five rubles and handed him the money.

He also made it clear to my mother that would have to buy my schoolbooks while the other children got them for free. She agreed to everything on his terms as long he permitted me to attend his school. Then he turned to me.

"What's your name?" he asked.

"Malke Sherman," I replied in a small voice.

"How old are you?" he asked, but I wasn't sure.

"She's seven years old," replied my mother.

When my mother left me, I was close to tears and felt like running after her. Here I was in a class full of non-Jewish children and my mother had just left me there. I felt their glances and heard their whispering which made me feel uncomfortable. I clutched at my seat and stared at the blackboard. I had never spoken or played with a gentile child before, as they lived on their farms completely isolated from the Jewish people.

The girls were all dressed alike. They all had long skirts and their heads were covered with colored kerchiefs.

Slowly I raised my eyes and looked around me. The room was enormous with three rows of seats and divided into three different grades. I was aware that many seats were empty. I could understand why parents kept their children back to work in the fields especially the bigger ones.

When the teacher came into the classroom, we all stood up to wish him a good morning. We continued to stand until he told us to sit down. His booming voice and stern face frightened me. I was afraid to move a muscle. I had no book or paper that first day, so I just sat there and listened as the teacher explained something that was on the blackboard.

Later, during lunch hour all the children trooped outside to play. I, too, went out to participate in their games, but they were jabbering in Russian and ignored me. I finally walked into the darkened classroom and watched them through the window, feeling alone and apart. I missed the security of the cheider and being with Jewish children, who spoke in Yiddish and allowed me to play with them. Later the students returned to the classroom, rosy-cheeked, and took their seats, still ignoring me.

Going home after school the children were rough and wild with each other. One boy pushed me, but the teacher noticed it and yelled at him to behave himself. He then made me wait until the whole class had cleared out, then he motioned for me to go home.

School hours were from eight-thirty in the morning till three in the afternoon. The worse offense was to be late or to break the silence. The punishment would be to stay for a whole hour on your knees.

I was a good student and my Russian teacher was pleased. "Horosho" he would often say to me. I liked school but I didn't have any friends. They stuck together and ignored me.

It seemed like the children resented me because they played all kinds of tricks on me. They would hide my overshoes, drop my coat on the floor and at other times someone would write something on the blackboard and tell the teacher that I wrote it.

I would be close to tears as I thought the teacher would punish me, but he ignored them. He also tried to make me feel at ease. Once he made me a monitor to make me feel important. It only made the children resent me more.

The girl who sat behind me seemed angry with me. Naively, I asked her why she was mad at me.

"You think you're a big shot because the teacher made you a monitor," she replied.

"But it's only for one day." I replied.

"It makes no difference, you don't belong here," she said.

I decided to ignore her remark.

"How is school?" my mother asked me one day.

"Ok mama."

I didn't want to tell her that the children were playing tricks on me. I was afraid that she would take me out of school if I tell her the truth, so I kept quiet.

Despite every thing, I began to like school and I would walk the mile in all kinds of weather. My mind was fast and I began to read and write well in Russian. "Look mama I got a hundred today" and I would show my paper to my mother with pride.

I was no longer afraid of my Russian teacher with his booming voice.

I became attached to him and adored him. I never thought of him as a gentile but as a friend. He took me under his wing and always watched out for me.

The girl, who sat next to me was about eight years old but no bigger than me. Her blond hair was braided and she wore a flowered kerchief. She was slightly more friendly then the rest. Her name was Tonia and she was quieter than the others so I took a liking to her.

I would let her use my inkwell when hers was dry or lend her my pen. One day Tonia spilled her ink and blamed me for it.

"Look what you did you dirty Szid!"

Hearing those words from the girl I liked was like an explosion to my pride. I knew that I had nothing to do with spilling her ink, but I didn't protest or deny that I had done anything. Her words cut deeply and I tried not to cry, but the tears just wouldn't stop. I had never encountered hatred before.

On the way home I kept hearing those terrible words, dirty Jew and wondered what they meant. I didn't understand hate and hostility. Later at home I examined myself in the mirror. I checked my hands and then my feet until I was fully reassured.

During dinner my mind was still confused. I knew that I was Jewish and that we celebrated different holidays. We also celebrated the Sabbath on Saturday instead of Sunday, but why should they hate us for that? I wondered. I don't hate them for being in churches and celebrating different holidays. I suddenly wondered what the Jews did to deserve such hate. I took my problem to my grandmother who lived with us and always read the Bible.

I walked down the hall and knocked on her door. When she answered, I came right to the point, "Bobeh, what is a Jew?"

My grandmother, a small, petite woman in her sixties invited me in.

"Come here and sit down near me," she said. Somehow I knew that she sensed my problem.

"A Jew is someone who lives by the Law that was given to us by our teacher, Moses."

"Where do the Jewish people come from, Bobeh?"

"They come from the children of Isaac who was the son of Abraham and Sarah. Malke, is there something wrong?"

I then told her of my experience with my classmate who called me a dirty Jew.

"There is no reason for all this hate," she said and sighed.

"Bobeh?"

"Yes, my child."

"Tell me about God."

"Malke, there is one God and all the people of the world are His children. He doesn't measure his love by what religion a person believes in."

My grandmother's words were soothing and calmed me, but I still wanted to find out why the girl called me a dirty Jew.

The following day during the lunch hour I asked Tonia why she didn't like me. She said to me, "because you're Jewish."

"Why don't you like the Jewish people?" I asked.

"Because they do bad things," she said.

"What kind of bad things?" I asked curiously.

"You really want to know?"

"Yes, I want to know," I replied.

"All right, I'll tell you. It's because the Jews kill little Christian children and use their blood for the Passover holiday. That's why there are brown spots on the matzah."

I tried to remember what the matzah looked like, and to my horror I realized that there were brown spots on the matzah when they came out of the oven.

"It's not true!" I retorted defensively. The brown spots are the burned part of the matzah," I explained.

But Tonia wouldn't accept that kind of reasoning.

"Why do you think that you are right?" I demanded.

"Because my mother told me so. Ask anyone in the classroom and see if they tell you different."

That night I could hardly eat my dinner. I kept seeing Tonia's accusing eyes. I wondered if there was some truth in it. Had my grandmother held something back? Again I took my problem to my grandmother and told her what the gentile girl said about the Jews.

"Nonsense, there isn't a word of truth in it! Her thinking is all wrong. Someone made up that terrible lie and told it to the children. I hope some day the Christians will draw a new image of our faith and a new way of thinking", she said sadly. "Jewish people have always been treated badly," she added.

"Why Bobeh?"

"I wish I knew the answer. This has been going on for centuries. Malke, let me read to you the historic story of Passover."

My grandmother picked the family Bible from the table and began to read the story of the Passover holiday. She described how the Jews had suffered as slaves in Egypt and how they were beaten for every little thing until a leader by the name of Moses finally brought them out of bondage.

As I listened I could see the wooden carts crossing the sea and the Pharaoh's terrified soldiers on horseback being swallowed up by the sea as the Jewish people were saved.

"This is why we put bitter herbs on the table on the Seders. It symbolizes the bitterness of the slavery which the Jews were under from the Egyptians," she explained.

"Bobeh, why do we have to eat matzah on Passover?"

"Because there was no time to wait for the yeast to rise, so they had to make matzah the fastest way."

My grandmother's words held meaning and it put my mind at rest. I grew a little older, a little wiser.

One day a man neatly dressed came into the classroom and said something to the teacher. I didn't pay attention until the man started to raise his voice. I wondered what was going on.

I looked up from my book and saw a tall man with a flushed face his brown eyes narrow and piercing. He seemed angry and threatening. He reminded me of a Cossack and my knees began to tremble.

No one knew what the argument was about and the incident was soon forgotten.

"Mama, I'm going to be in a Christmas play," I told my mother one day.

"A Jewish girl in a Christmas play?"

" I'm going to recite a poem" I was trembling with excitement In my fantasy I saw myself standing up on a platform and reciting the poem for everyone to hear.

"When is the play going to be?"

"Sometime in December. Mama, can I have a new dress?"

"Yes," she replied.

I was dancing for joy.

Every single day I studied the poem I was supposed to memorize. I would have the book in front of me when I ate or slept. In no time I had memorized the verses of the poem. I would have my sister, Goldie, hold my book and I would recite the poem with gestures as if I were standing on the platform in school.

It was a dry, frosty November morning. Snowflakes big as a ruble were coming down one by one. I got up real early that morning, I washed and dressed and hardly ate my breakfast. I was full of excitement. It was the day of the rehearsal for the Christmas play.

"Malke", said my father, "you ought to stay home today. It looks as if it's going to be a real blizzard." The wind was rising whipping the flakes about.

"Your father is right ", said my mother as she glanced out the window. "It's a bad day even for a dog to be out."

"But, Mama, I must go to school to day I have to rehearse my poem for the play."

"Well, if you must go, be careful."

She made sure that I had my overshoes on, my woolen gloves and a kerchief on my head. She gave me my lunch of bread and jelly and an apple. I took my books and left.

Outside the wind almost picked me up. The air was so sharp that I could hardly breathe. My eyes began to tear up, and blurred. Snow soon covered me from head to foot. I had to walk slowly and I was afraid that I might be late. I tried to hurry, accidentally ran into a snowdrift and fell, dropping all of my books and my lunch. I got up and brushed off the snow that almost covered me, retrieved my books and lunch, but I couldn't find my pen. I was upset but I decided to continue walking.

Soon my hands and feet became numb with the cold, but I finally got to the school. I walked up the stairs and was about to open the door when

I noticed that it was slightly ajar. I thought some student might have been careless and had left it open. I opened the door wider and walked in, closing the door after me, as I knew how strict my teacher was about the door, heat was precious.

There wasn't a sound anywhere except for my own footsteps and heavy breathing. That was very odd as there should have been more people. I walked over to my classroom and listened at the door, but I heard nothing. Slowly I opened the door and looked in. It was dark and no one seemed to be there. I felt disappointed. It must have been the blizzard that kept everyone from coming to school. I was about to turn when my eyes caught sight of something. I took a step forward and my heart froze. I was looking at the body of my Russian teacher in the eerie silence of the cold classroom. I knew that he was dead because he was laying in a pool of blood.

I backed out of the room and then ran from the building. My tears mingled with the snow as I trudged home. The horrible sight of my Russian teacher seemed to waver right in front of me. The snow kept falling and the icy wind tore at me, but I didn't feel it.

I was numb with the cold and my hands and feet were half frozen by the time I finally got home. My parents were surprised to see me back from school so early.

"Was the school closed because of the storm?" my mother asked, but I couldn't answer. Tears kept running down my face.

"Why are you crying?" she asked as she was removing my kerchief and my snow-covered gloves and coat. She took my wet gloves off my fingers and massaged my ice-cold hands. She blew on them with the air from her mouth to get them warm.

I leaned my head on her breast and sobbed. "Oh, mama, oh mama," I cried.

My mother looked at me with concern in her eyes, "What is it? Why are you crying like that?"

"My teacher is dead," I finally blurted out. My parents were aghast.

"What are you saying?" My father asked. I finally told them between sobs about the experience in school. I was now crying as if my heart was breaking. My mother wiped my tear-swollen face and tried to calm me.

"Perhaps he is only hurt?" my mother questioned.

"No, mama, he's dead," I replied, knowing that there was no way that he was still alive.

Several days later, long haired priests, monks, and deacons garbed in their flowing black robes and wearing long chain crosses carried icons, banners, and heavy crosses, praying and singing "Rest Eternal" as they slowly marched to the orthodox church. Peasants crossed themselves as they passed us by. Some joined in out of curiosity and asked, "Who is being buried?"

"Andre Gorky, the school-master."

In the church I was the only Jew. I stood among the gentiles and followed them around the coffin that stood in the center.

"Do vstrechi," (farewell) I whispered in Russian and left the church.

I never returned to that Russian school again. It was only afterward that I remembered the man who had come to the school one day and argued with the teacher.

I was too young to understand it then, but there was a rumor that Andre Gorky was killed because he was kind to a little Jewish student, me.

A PRAYER FOR MAMA

It was the year after the Russian revolution when an epidemic of typhus broke out and swept the town. Many of our neighbors became ill with the horrible disease and died, including my Uncle Pinnie. Some were fortunate enough to recover despite that there were no doctors in town except for a practitioner who had never taken any formal medical training.

The felsher, a Ukrainian, was a tall, stocky man with a round face, thick eyebrows, and a drooping mustache. Even though he didn't have any formal training, the sick people called him anyway. He would look at them and then prescribe some kind of medicine, which might be nothing more than peppermint water for a cough.

My mother worried about us children catching the disease so she made us wear little sacks with a string through it around our necks. They were filled with camphor and garlic. People ran away from us, but it seemed to help.

One day I came home from a friend's house and my grandmother met me at the door with a silencing finger to her lips. "Shh… Malke don't make any noise. Be quiet, Mama is not feeling well."

I saw my father pacing back and forth through our corridor, his face pale. My two older sisters walked on their tiptoes and whispered. My younger brother was crying.

That was strange. I didn't know that mothers got sick. But something in my grandmother's manner and tone of her voice told me that my mother was seriously ill.

I softly tiptoed to the bedroom where my mother lay. With my hand on the knob, I slowly opened the door. I had the shock of my life, as I had never seen mama look so pale and helpless in bed in the middle of the day. An ice bag covered most of her head her breathing was heavy and her eyes were closed. Her face looked as white as the sheet that she was laying on.

"Mama, Mama," I whispered, but she didn't reply. I softly closed the door and walked back into the kitchen where my grandmother was preparing dinner. She placed a bowl of soup and a piece of bread on the table for me to eat, but I had lost my appetite.

"Why don't you eat your soup?" she asked.

"I'm not hungry," I replied.

Later the practitioner was called. We stood watching him hoping for a miracle, but after taking a look at my mother, he shook his head. "She has typhus, there is nothing I can do'" he said, his eyes full of sympathy.

We were all horrified. My sisters and my grandmother began to cry. My father seemed stunned. With Typhus, we knew that there was very little chance for her to recover.

My mother's illness became a real family crisis as we depended so much on her. No matter, how bad things were, she kept us from starvation.

Now things were at a stand still. No one could take her place. The whole house seemed desolate and sad.

An awful fear clutched at my heart. My mother might die and it frightened me. I just couldn't equate my mother with death.

"Bobeh, is mama going to die?" I asked in a trembling voice.

"God forbid, you mustn't think like that," she replied. "Malke, people do get sick and sometimes they die, but we must pray so she can live."

Every single night I would say my prayers and talk intimately with God. I told Him how badly my little brother needed mama, how we all needed her.

But despite my praying, my mother was sinking into death. My grandmother spent an hour each morning in the synagogue praying for my mother's recovery.

"Bobeh, can I go with you to the synagogue?" I asked one morning. She nodded without a word. My patched up coat didn't protect me from the icy wind in March as I followed her through the gray, slushy streets.

The synagogue, the only one in town, was an old building with tall stained windows from which nearly all the color had faded.

Inside the temple, it was cold, damp and dark. I followed my grandmother to one of the pews and sat down. She picked up a prayer book from one of the tables and sat down next to me. She opened the holy book, leafing through the pages, and found the place she wanted. She began to pray in a loud voice.

"Almighty God," she prayed, "Show mercy to the children who need their mother, let my daughter live." Tears ran down her face as she completely forgot that I was there.

Her praying provoked a feeling of sadness such as I had never experienced before. I suddenly felt old and bewildered for my seven years of age. I cried without a sound.

Then a miracle happened. A new doctor came into town, he was our last hope. It seemed an eternity until he arrived at our home. We all stood anxiously behind him while he examined my mother. When he finished he told us that she was far-gone, but he'd try his best. He gave her an injection and wrote something on a piece of paper.

"Get this at the drugstore and give her the medicine every two hours. I'll be back next week," he promised.

My two sisters took turns watching mama. Then on the third day after giving her the medicine she opened her eyes for the first time.

She had passed the crises and we knew that the worst was over. The following day mama gave us a weak smile. Whatever the new doctor did for my mother, it helped her and she was recovering. Two days later when I came home from school my mother sat up and my grandmother fed her some soup. It made me realize how near we came to losing mama and it made me cherish her so much more.

OUR JOURNEY TO FREEDOM

One day we received a letter from my older brother Hershel, who was married and lived in the United States. In his letter he urged us to immigrate to America. He said he would send us all the money we would need for the journey.

My two older sisters, Goldie and Laike, danced for joy when they heard the news of our journey. My younger brother Shloime threw his cap in the air and ran outside to tell his friends the good news. "Hey, Motle," he called out, "We're going to America!" Then he ran to his other friends to tell them the news.

As for me, my mind was working overtime. I could see lots of sweets and new clothes instead of the homemade dresses I wore which my mother had cut from my sisters old clothes.

But to our disappointment my father put my brother's letter down on the table without a word.

"What do you think?" my mother asked him.

"I don't know, Raizl," my father replied. "I can't see the sense in leaving a perfectly good home and starting our life in a new country with a strange language? Besides, America is a sinful land, the Jews are really easy going there. They don't keep up the Sabbath like they should, they also eat non-kosher meat and I've heard that they even eat on Yom Kippur." My father also found personal reasons, "and I don't want to leave my only sister," he added.

My mother frowned. "Why do you want to stay in a land where people despise you and who constantly call you Zhid. They don't consider you as a human being capable of thinking and feeling. There is our daily fear of being attacked by the dreadful Cossacks or by the drunken peasants. What future is there for our children in this country when schools are forbidden to them by the Russian government because we're Jews?" she replied.

My father stood up and began pacing our darkened corridor. I could see that he was thinking. My two sisters, my mother, my brother and I watched him as our whole life depended on it.

After a few minutes he stopped in front of my mother, "Look, Raizl if it'll make you happy to live in the golden land you dream about, then we'll go."

My sister Laike let out a scream that scared my mother, "Papa, do you mean it?" she asked full of excitement.

"Yes, I mean it. Your mother is right, we must make a change."

The following week we received another letter and in it was money, twenty-five dollars in American money.

The same day we began to plan. There were so many things to do. Sewing, mending, selling some of the household items, and the house itself was just some of the things on our to-do list.

A few days later we found out that one of our relatives was leaving in about two weeks, and was willing to take my two sisters along with him.

My sisters were so overjoyed that my parents had given them permission to leave. "We'll follow later when we're ready," my father said. My mother sewed some money in the lining of one of my sister's coat. After their bags were packed with the necessary things for their trip, they finally left. I didn't mind. I'll have the bed all to myself, I thought. I wished that my brother would've gone with them as we were always fighting.

Our house was now crowded with people buying things. The news that we were leaving for America spread like wild fire. Our neighbors didn't like us leaving, as my father was their beloved cantor.

They would also come to my father with a problem and ask his advice on many things, even marital problems. Our house was always open to friends and relatives. Our samovar would always steam and my mother would serve tea and her famous poppy-seed cookies. Now we were leaving them for good and some of our neighbors were crying.

Our house was full of activity for our journey, but I wasn't much help to my mother, neither was my father. He wanted her to leave every thing, but my mother wouldn't part with a lot of things. Especially her featherbeds and the feather-pillows which she had made with her own hands.

My wardrobe was made of my mothers white tablecloths dyed blue. My coat came from my grandmother's wide velvet skirt that had been in her trunk for a decade.

Hiem, the shoemaker, measured my feet and made me a pair of shoes. They were shiny and they squeaked as I proudly paraded back and forth in front of our house, showing them off to the neighborhood kids who surrounded me and asked me all kinds of questions.

"Is your brother rich?" one of them asked.

"I heard America is full of gold," another one said, "That's why they call it the Golden Land."

"Here," I said to my playmate, Nadia. "You can have my Russian book."

Nadia was my closest girlfriend. We played, danced together and shared everything, including food.

"I'll never see you again," she said.

"No," I replied, "but I'll write to you, I promise."

It took us over six months before we were ready to leave.

When we finally applied for an exit visa, the Russian government denied us the right to emigrate. My mother spent days pleaded with the Russian Officials to allow us to leave the country, but to no avail.

My parents by now had become frantic. "What are we going to do?" my mother asked my father during dinner.

"There is only one thing that we can do, we'll leave the country whether they like it or not."

"But it's dangerous", my mother replied. "If we get caught it would mean twenty years in prison."

"Raizl, there is no other way, we'll have to take the risk."

We secretly had our passports, birth certificates, and other necessary papers made by a man we had known and could trust. Of course we had to be extremely careful so the Russian government wouldn't find out or we could've been in serious trouble. Our transportation tickets, therefore, could only start at a point in Poland across the Russian boundaries.

But first we had to get to a last town before the Russian and Austrian border. A town named Shipotovka. There we would stay until it was time for us to steal across the border to a town name Brody.

Luckily we got in touch with a relative who lived in Shipotovka, which was about ten miles away from Meropol.

My Aunt wrote back that she'd give us a room to stay in and the use of her kitchen.

We had everything packed and ready to go. Even a peasant was hired to take us to the town.

On the day of our departure all our friends and relatives surrounded us. There were embraces, tears, kisses, and the promises of writing. My father's only sister wept in my father's arms. "You're the only brother and family I have in the world, "she cried.

"I'll write to you, Haye," he promised as he embraced her.

"Please don't forget to write and let us know how things are in America," they pleaded.

The mothers to be embraced my grandmother. They didn't like to see her go as she was a midwife and the young mothers depended on her so much.

At last we climbed into the deep, narrow wagon with the two stout horses. The driver sat in the front holding the reins, his back towards us. "Vio!" he called out to the horses hitting them with a whip. I could hardly see them, and I felt as if some magic force was pulling me. For the first time in my life I was going to another town. I had never been anywhere else. I was full of curiosity and kept looking at everything we passed.

I sat in the back of the wagon clutching the bag of food in my hands that my mother prepared for the trip. I had no idea what the food was, but it was pretty heavy.

The wagon squeaked and groaned as it rattled over the cobblestone streets. We now passed a jumble of houses, and then we took a bridge over a river. The railroad track was visible over a field on the right side of the road. The passing of the train thrilled me and I watched with great satisfaction, and curiosity as it sped by leaving a trail of smoke behind.

Then we went past the market, where the peasants brought their product in their horse drawn wagons during the summertime in the early morning.

By noon it was crowded with sellers and buyers. I would often follow mama to the market, where she would buy strawberries or other things and always bargain with the farmers. Of course, no one paid the asking price there was always bargaining going on all the time.

We were now on the outskirts. We rode past huts with straw roofs, and pastures where cows and horses grazed. Suddenly we heard galloping hoofs and a harsh voice shouting. "Stoy! Stoy!" Our driver stopped the horses and waited until the three horsemen caught up to us. They were dressed in casual clothes and carried rifles over their shoulders.

"Where are you going?" one of then asked in Russian.

"We're moving to Shepetovka," my mother replied.

"What for?" the tallest one asked.

"To live near our loved ones."

"Do you have a permit?"

"No, we didn't know that we needed one," my mother replied again.

"You're lying!" he shouted, "you're leaving the country!"

"No, please believe us," my grandmother spoke up. "I'm old and sick, I want to live near my other daughter."

My father couldn't speak a word in Russian so he just sat there without saying a word.

I could see that the three horsemen were holding a meeting, talking to each other quietly as to what to do with us.

"We'll follow you and see if you are telling us the truth."

They did. They followed us all the way to the to the town of Shepetovka and to my Aunt's house. When they saw that people were coming out of the house to welcome us and help us with our belongings by carrying them into the house, the horsemen were finally convinced and galloped away. My parents sighed with relief.

We entered a house of only four rooms. The kitchen was painted green and she had the same oven that we had.. We followed my Aunt to a room with two beds and a table in the middle. "This is your room, you can stay as long as you have to," she said.

The room looked big enough for us, until we moved in there with all our belongings. We could hardly move about. My mother started to look through what was left of our possessions and found that some of her things were missing. The copper kettle, frying pans, and other things that she needed for cooking were nowhere to be found. She was almost in tears.

My father shook his head. "We'll buy new ones in America," he said, "What do you need all those things for? They're not worth dragging along on so far of a trip."

But my mother was upset about it. "I took them because I knew that I'll need them for cooking. Now I'll have to borrow the very same pots and pans."

The little town was no bigger than Meropol. There was a handful of Jews living close together. The Gentiles lived on the outskirts on their farms. My parents didn't waste any time. They began to look around for some one to guide us across the Russian border almost immediately after we arrived.

It was almost impossible to find a guide. If anyone was caught smuggling Jews over the border, he'd be subjected to ten years in prison. After several days of searching, we heard of a peasant who was willing to guide us across the border if we paid him twenty-five rubles in advance.

We knew nothing about him, but we had no choice, but to trust him. He seemed like he was in his early thirties and he looked like a quiet man.

"Did you guide someone before?" my mother asked.

"No, but I'm willing to take the chance." he replied. My parents looked at each other. They weren't sure if they could trust him. But they had no choice. They paid him the money he asked for.

"What are we going to do with all our belongings?" my mother asked Ivan.

"Dress as peasants we won't have any trouble passing, they don't bother the Gentile people." he replied.

Two days later he came with his horse-drawn wagon in the early morning to pick us up.

"Your husband's beard would give him away, he'll have to go with my other Jewish group."

"We'll, I think Ivan is right, you go ahead and I'll meet you later in Brody. But make sure that you give him the correct address so I'll know where you'll be staying," my father said.

My father was about to pick me up and put me in the wagon when

I changed my mind. "I want to stay with papa," I exclaimed. My parents looked at me with surprise and concern.

"Malke, you must come with us in the wagon. It's too far for a little girl to walk," my mother said.

"Your mother is right," my grandmother agreed.

"Mama, I want to stay with papa, too," my younger brother Shloime said. I knew that I made a problem for my parents, but I still wanted to stay with my father. In my mind I saw adventure and the promise of interesting things to see.

"Let her stay with me. It's only about ten miles or so."

My mother didn't like the idea, but gave in. When I said goodbye to my mother, she kissed me, something she had never done before. "You haven't changed your mind, Malke?" she asked.

"No, mama'" I replied.

But when they left I suddenly missed my mother. My father and I ate our lunch in silence. We had to wait for Ivan to come back and let us know that they had successfully passed the border.

But as the hours passed and there was no sign of our guide, my father began to worry. He kept watching the clock; sure that mother and the rest of our family had been caught. After what seemed like an eternity we heard my aunt callout, "Ivan is here!"

We were never so glad to see anyone before. He gave us the address from the rooming house where my mother was staying, then he picked us up in his wagon and took us to his farm on the outskirts where the other group was waiting. There were three couples, plus two single men, my father and me, making ten of us not including our guide.

My father shook hands with all of them. "Sholom, Alehem."

"Sholom, Alehem," they replied in return. They seemed friendly and were eager to know us better. They all had the same story. The Russians wouldn't allow them to leave so they were leaving on their own. "But your little girl," a woman said, "won't she get tired by hiking all those miles to the border?" I could see that she was concerned that I might give them a hard time.

"I won't get tired." I replied, not liking what the woman had said.

Then Ivan spoke up, "Folks, we'll start the hike tomorrow at six in the morning. I have no place for you to sleep except for my barn."

Later we bought milk from Ivan and had it for supper. During the meal we got to know each other.

Later Ivan led us to his barn with a lit lantern. The fowl smell of dung hit my nostrils, but we all stretched out on the straw strewn floor. I heard the munching of the cows and ever so often I would hear them moo. It was strange sleeping in a barn with cows, but I decided that it was fun.

The straw was cold and damp and I was cold during the night, my coat couldn't keep me warm. I must have fallen asleep because the next thing I heard was the voice of Ivan our guide. "Stavy!" he shouted and left the barn door open. It was still very early and my eyes refused to open. I eventually got up, washed, and ate something.

With bundles on our backs we entered a misty, dingy forest that few people would dare to traverse. The forest came alive with the chirping of birds while the small animals scurried for cover. We made our way around overturned and broken branched and wild grass that was taller than my head and wet with dew. Twigs snapped under our feet while squirrels ran up and down trees. There was the occasional hooting of owls. A flock of geese flew over our heads with a honking sound that echoed for miles.

We walked through streams edged with wild vegetation. At times the trails were so narrow that we had to raise our arms to ward off the whipping branches to avoid so that they didn't scratch our faces. At other times we walked through mud so deep that my father had to carry me piggy-back, as I was always stuck and had to be pulled. Eventually, I began to tire and kept tugging at my father's sleeve. "How much more do we have to walk?"

"A little while longer," he replied patiently. I felt like a grown up as I followed my father and the others. But I was so little that the tall grass was taller than me. My father would always stop and made sure that he could see me.

After what seemed like an eternity, we sat on the ground and rested while my father and I lunched on the food that my aunt had prepared for us. We had cooked potatoes, hard-boiled eggs, onions and bread. Everyone lunched as they rested.

We then resumed our hiking. It was getting harder and harder for me to keep up with the grown-ups. I stumbled and fell several times.

Ever so often our guide would pause, his fingers on his lips to warn us to keep quiet. He would strain his ears listening, and then he would motion for us to move on.

We were always conscious of the danger of being caught. The hike, which was only about ten or twelve miles, took all day because of the many difficulties of the forest. Mud, streams, and overturned old trees, made it seem like we had been walking forever.

Then, almost before we knew it the day was gone, it was getting darker and gloomy in the forest. One of the men lit a cigarette and coughed. Our guide quickly snatched it out of his hand. "You fool! Do you want us to get caught?"

It was quiet except for the occasional owl that hooted, the singing crickets, or the sound of frogs or other animals. I held on to my father's hand as we walked now very slowly because of the darkness. Later the moon came out and lit up the area like a flashlight. A river came into view and we stopped. I wondered why.

"We must swim across!" our guide said.

"Swim across?" one woman asked. They were all terrified as nobody had a bathing suit in their possessions.

"Isn't there another way?" one of the men asked.

"I'm afraid not. Well, there is, but it's too dangerous. Do you people know how to swim?" our guide asked.

Most of them knew how to swim, but the women wouldn't get undressed.

"Look, we can't lose any more time," one of the men said. We must make it across the border while it's still dark otherwise it will be too dangerous. Come on forget how you look and let's get into the river and swim across."

But the women wouldn't budge. No one made a move to remove their clothes. The full moon cast it's silver sheen across the river making the water seem dark and deep. I stood at the edge of the river, no one paying any attention to me.

Suddenly, to the astonishment to everyone including myself, I got undressed and jumped into the water. Our guide picked up my clothes and held them up high with one hand while guiding me with the other. The water was icy and it stung my skin. It was also deep and I kept sinking and swallowing water, which made me gag and cough. At one time I sank below the surface and thought for sure that I would drown, but Ivan had a good grip on my waist and coaxed me to move my feet.

Finally, we reached the bank of the river. He handed me my clothes and turned back to help the others. When I looked back, I saw that the women were in the water although they were still wearing their slips.

My teeth chattered as I dressed. Surprisingly my clothes were still dry. Soon everybody had crossed the river and was getting dressed. The women hid behind the bushes to remove their wet slips and finally got dressed.

"Let's rest awhile," our guide suggested as he flopped down on the ground. He pulled a vodka bottle out of his pocket, uncorked it with his teeth, and gulped it down as if it were water. He stopped long enough to wipe his mouth with the sleeve of his shirt. As he drank he became very talkative, which surprised us all, as he had been cautioning us all to be silent. Now he couldn't stop talking and began to hiccup and belch.

He changed from a nice, quiet man to a drunken man we didn't know and couldn't trust. This was a problem none of us expected. He finally stood up, but he looked unstable. He was in no condition to guide us to the border.

"Ivan, take it easy we have a big job to do," my father said to him.

"Go away, Zhid," he shouted and swung his bottle narrowly missing Misha's head. Not only did we fear the border patrol, but now our drunken guide as well.

"Oh my God," one of the women sighed and wrung her hands," what are we going to do?"

"Calm yourself, Fraidl we have no time for hysterics." Misha said.

Ivan's eyes glazed as he stared at us, "You Jews find your own way to the border" he said. Then he staggered away, finally disappearing in the brush.

We all stood there stunned, one woman began to cry. "He took all our money," she exclaimed.

"Listen, folks, there is no time to waste. Pretty soon it will begin to get light and it will be too dangerous to do anything." Misha said. He took command. "I have a good idea where the border is, it's only about a mile away."

All around us lay darkness and the unknown. We didn't know where to turn.

"Let's make a chain by holding hands so we won't lose anyone." Misha suggested.

We walked slowly, almost as if fearing to take the next step. I held on to my father's hand very tightly because I was afraid of the darkness. Several times I tripped and almost fell. We were all praying for guidance and for us to get across the border safely. The moon was fading it was now getting light, so we had to be extra careful.

After walking and stumbling we finally paused and looked around us. "There it is," Joshua, the youngest man, whispered.

"Shh," Misha warned. We came upon a wall of barbed wire, but the men quickly held it up and parted the wires for others to get through. One of the women stumbled and gave a low cry as she fell.

Suddenly we heard a shot, then another, and another. We froze in our tracks. Within minutes we were surrounded by a group of soldiers. I saw the gleam of rifles pointing at us and lanterns shining in our faces.

We were soon marched to a wooden dwelling where a Russian with a little brush mustache barked all kinds of questions at us.

"Are you spies? Where are you going? You could be heavily punished for treason," he said. "You better tell the truth, it will be easier on you!"

No one answered the questions he threw at us.

After the endless hours of questions, he finally shouted out an order and we were marched down hill to a clay, one room hut.

Inside it was dark and smelled of decayed leaves and mildew. We were all huddled together in the one small room. We stood around wordlessly still in shock. We couldn't believe that we were caught and now imprisoned. We had taken a risk and lost. I heard the women crying and the men trying to calm them.

"Papa, I'm afraid."

"Malke, there is nothing to worry about. If they send us back, we'll come some other time."

My father tried to make light of things, but I knew better. In my mind I pictured them sending us to Siberia or may be even shooting us for treason.

I felt so exhausted that I fell asleep on the bare floor. When I opened my eyes, everybody was asleep including my father. I stood up and looked out the small dirty window of our prison. The mist had settled and a slow rising sun appeared over the horizon. The country was now visible and I could make out crooked chimneys from which black smoke was belching. It must be where mama is staying, I thought.

Suddenly, I had a strong desire to see my mother to tell her of our capture, as she'd never know where we were. I was sure that we'd be sent to Siberia soon.

I checked the door and to my surprise, it wasn't locked. Without glancing at my father or at anyone else in our group, I opened the door wider and ran out.

I quickly dropped to the ground and listened. I saw no one, so I stood up and ran towards the road only to be blocked by a wall of barbed wire. Without hesitation I got underneath it and wriggled myself through, scarcely aware of the sharp barbs that scratched my hands and caught in my clothes and hair.

When I reached the other side, I crouched behind a tree and waited. When I didn't see anyone, I ran wildly toward the brush. I felt a surge of panic when I thought I heard the voice of a soldier calling after me, but I didn't stop. My heart pounded with terror as I expected a bullet to pierce my back at any moment. I could see myself falling to the ground wounded or even dead.

I hurled myself into the tall wild grass and lay there panting. My heart beating so hard that it shook my whole body. I was too afraid to even move a muscle. Suddenly I wanted to sneeze. I tried to suppress it, but couldn't. I sneezed once, then twice. I was sure that I was doomed, but it was quiet, I didn't hear the sound of any boots or shouting.

I raised my head cautiously, and I saw no one around me. I stood up and looked around me to make sure that I was safe. Without looking back I hurried down a hillside across a meadow and found myself in a strange, unfamiliar, rural village of clay huts, small houses, and gardens of growing vegetables.

It was still early morning, no later than six o'clock. The village was still deserted. A rooster shouted out a loud cock-a-doodle-do. A dog barked furiously from a fenced yard as I passed. I began to run, I was always afraid of dogs. I passed houses on both sides of the street. I went by a courtyard where chickens were cackling and pecking grain from the earth. Doors opened and closed.

I was very fearful as I walked and kept looking over my shoulder. I had a strange feeling that the soldiers were following me.

As I walked I came face to face with a woman who carried wooden buckets swinging from a yoke on her shoulders. I knew she was going to the well for water. She wore a bright flowered kerchief and was walking barefoot.

"Can you tell me how to get to the town of Brody?" I asked.

The woman studied my face and mud-splashed clothes. "Where did you come from?" she asked suspiciously.

I quickly moved away. I was afraid that she would figure out that I was a criminal. I had run away from the prison at the Russian border and that made me a delinquent despite my young age. I didn't know whom I could trust. I passed several people who stared at me, but I was afraid to stop and ask them how to get to the city.

I kept walking and saw an aged farmer working by the roadside. I decided to talk to him. I crossed the street where he was, and greeted him in Russian.

"Could you tell me how to get to the town of Brody?"

He stood and stared at me. "Where are your parents?" he asked.

His tone of voice scared me, but I braved myself. "My parents are with my grandmother who is very sick. I'm supposed to meet them there," I fibbed hoping that he would believe me.

"What a shame," he replied but I wondered if he really believed me as he gave me directions.

"Follow that road, make a right at the first road you come too, and then you'll see a wooden bridge. Turn left and it would take you straight to the city of Brody."

"Spacebo," I said and I quickly walked away. I was sure that I wouldn't have any trouble finding my mother, now that I got the directions to the city.

Suddenly I came face to face with a soldier. My heart began to beat with fright. But to my amazement he passed me by without a second glance. With a sigh of relief I continued walking only to run into a barracks full of soldiers. Some were outside polishing their boots, while others were cleaning their rifles. Again my heart began to beat. But they too, ignored me. I didn't look back until I was clear out of the village.

My shoes were soggy and caked with mud. They felt so heavy and hurt my feet. I dropped to the side of the road and removed my shoes and stockings only to discover an open blister on each heel. I couldn't put my shoes on again so I decided to walk barefooted. The air felt good on my feet but I tried to put my shoes on again as I didn't like to walk barefoot as I might hurt myself. But when I tried to put them back on, they wouldn't fit. I now had no choice but walk barefoot. Carrying my muddy shoes, I had to walk very slowly as the road was unpaved and difficult to walk on. There were roots and stones, which were rough underneath my feet. Once I stumbled and almost fell. The roughness of the road slowed me down and I was sorry that I had taken my shoes off.

I was alone on a long lonely road in a strange land, miles away from home. I didn't have my mother, or father to guide and protect me. In all my ten years of life I had never been further from home than the school. But somehow I wasn't afraid. It was still early morning and I was headed to the town where I would find my mother. I didn't know the address of the rooming house where she was staying, but I was going to find her anyway. Back home in Meropol we always knew when a stranger came into town.

My left hand that carried my shoes felt lighter, and no wonder, I had lost one of my shoes. I was too far away to go back, so I dropped the other one, what good is one shoe? I was hoping my mother wouldn't scold me as they were made by one of our local shoemakers before we left for our journey.

I don't know how it happened, but I found myself in a deserted area. I turned and went down the hill thinking that it was the road that I had come on, but instead I went deeper into the wilderness.

I surveyed the countryside. The trees looked like monstrous creatures about to swallow me up. The village and the people vanished as if they had been erased from the earth.

I told myself not be scared, sooner or later some one will come along and help me. But there wasn't a human being to be seen. It was deathly still except for the faint sounds of the buzzing insects and small wild animals. As I walked, a flock of wild birds flew low over my head making a honking sound. I thought I heard footsteps, but there was only a woodpecker on a tree.

It was beginning to get hot and the sun was burning my face and my eyes. My feet hurt, but I kept moving, I was afraid to stop. I was becoming thirsty, but there were no streams anywhere. By now my stomach hurt from hunger so I looked among the bushes for berries, but there were bees and flies so I walked away.

Once my mother said that God is always with us and I suddenly felt that I wasn't alone. God is going to help me, I thought. I noticed that the sky was getting cloudy and it felt muggy, I removed my coat and threw it over my other arm.

I was beginning to tire and decided to rest awhile. All kinds of frightening thoughts passed my mind. I'll perish and my parents would never know what had happened to me. In all the entire ten years of my life I had never been further away from home than the school. Now I had left my father behind and became a traveler alone in strange, unfamiliar land.

A deep longing for my mother overtook me. I saw her sweet face in front of me singing the cradlesong that she sang to me when I was three years old. I still remembered it.

In The Oven
In the oven burns a little flame,
And it's hot in the room.
And the teacher drills the little children
In the alphabet,
And the teacher drills the little children in the alphabet.
Pay attention, children, Remember, dear ones,
What you study here,
Repeat once again,
And then again
Komets A-Ief O!

I tried to sing it in my small soprano voice, but no sound came out. I gave up and sang it in my mind. After resting for a while I stood up and walked again. Finally, I came upon a farm stretching over many acres of land. There were blooming trees, growing potatoes, cucumbers, beets, and cabbage patches.

My stomach hurt from hunger as I remembered that I hadn't eaten since the day before. I took an apple from a tree but it was green and sour so I threw it away. My eyes searched for someone to come along but all I saw were more acres of corn.

I became so tired that I could hardly take another step. Blisters appeared on the soles of my feet. I limped as I walked and cried with pain. My legs could hardly carry me much further but I resolved not to rest. Perhaps... perhaps... I'll find a way.

As I walked, I saw a stick a on the side of the road and I was about to pick it up when it moved. I jumped with fright and embraced a tree. It was a small snake.

After that experience I kept my eyes on the road. My heart pounded with exhaustion. I became weak and dazed. I collapsed on the side of the road, my arms clutching my frail body and I began to cry.

I was trapped and I knew that I was in terrible danger and I began to worry about my fate. I saw myself dead and nobody would find my body. I must have dozed off as I was startled by water on my face. I opened my eyes and I didn't remember where I was. Then the familiar terror came back. I glanced at the sky. It was dark and cloudy as if a gray curtain had been drawn across it. The sun was completely gone and the wilderness seemed more frightening than ever.

Pink flashes of lightning lit the sky like a bowl of fire followed by the roar of thunder. Then it began to rain a real heavy rain as if a lake came down pouring from the sky. I stood up but felt dizzy and weak. I put my hands out for some water and moistened my lips. Somehow the rain made me feel better. I became drenched to the skin but it cooled me off and satisfied some of my thirst.

Suddenly the rain stopped and the sun came out again. But the ground was so muddy that I had to climb to a higher ground. I was moving down hill when I saw cows and horses grazing. My heart began to beat with excitement. That meant that there must be people near by. My eyes searched for huts or houses when I saw a sign on a post. I limped over and there was big letters written in Polish, "One mile to Brody." Then, my eyes caught sight of a wooden bridge.

I felt as if I got wings to my feet as I ignored my blisters and swollen feet. I felt happy and safe as I moved toward the city of Brody. God guided me to the right path, I thought. I passed houses, gardens, and people, and it made me feel better knowing that I was going in the right direction.

Limping, dirty, exhausted, and starved; I finally reached the city of Brody.

I stood on the sidewalk and didn't know where to turn. I wanted to meet Jewish people who spoke in Yiddish, but I only saw Polish people and I wanted to ask one of them where the Jewish people were located, but I didn't know the language. Then I saw a man with a beard walking towards me. He seemed in a hurry, but I stopped him. "I'm looking for Jewish people."

"There is a Jewish delicatessen store about two blocks down," he replied and hurried away. I slowly crossed the street and slowly moved toward where he had signaled to. My feet hurt so much that I could hardly put my feet down on the cement sidewalk. People stared at my mud-splashed clothes and mud-caked feet. My uncombed hair was flying in my face. But I didn't care; I wanted to get to the Jewish store as soon as possible. My head ached, and I felt dizzy.

When I reached the store I had to lean on the wall for support. After a few minutes I peered into the open door and saw a man customer and a woman with grayish hair waiting on him and they spoke in Yiddish. A man with a white apron also gray was setting a table for the next customer. I waited until the customer left the store then I dragged myself inside. The smell of food made me dizzy.

"What do you want?" the man asked me in Polish.

"I, I am Jewish," I blurted out in Yiddish. Then my knees suddenly gave way, and I blacked out.

The next thing I knew I was sitting on a chair and the woman was pressing a glass of water to my lips, while the man was wiping my face with a wet cloth. They put hot soup, bread, and a glass of sweet tea on the table.

"Don't talk little girl until you have something in your stomach," the woman said.

Although I was dizzy from hunger, I could hardly swallow it. After I ate a few spoons of the soup, I began to feel better. My hands trembled from weakness and exhaustion. When I had rested for a while, I told them how we were caught by the Russian border patrol and about my running away, from the prison. I also told them how taking the wrong road had gotten me lost. I began to cry.

"Poor child," the woman said. "What made you do a thing like that?"

"I wanted to find my mother. She left before my father and me because she had all of our belongings."

"Do you know where she's staying?"

"No, I have no idea, but if it helps, her name is Raizle."

"There are lot's of women name Raizle in town," the man said smiling. "What's your name?"

"Malke."

"How old are you?"

"I think I'm ten."

"Lazor, do you think we could help her father in some way?" the woman asked.

"Bluma, the only one who could help her father and the others, is Rabbi Marcus. Tell me Malke, does your father have any money?"

I didn't know if my father had any money or not, but I still said yes to everything.

"We'll need money to buy the border patrol off. Reb-Marcus does it for a good deed, but he needs the money to help your father and the rest of your group." Lazor explained. "Come Malke, let's go, we mustn't lose any more time," Lazor said. Then he added, "Malke don't walk too close, I don't want people to get suspicious."

I was still weak and the bottom of my feet hurt more than ever, but I tried to keep up with him. We walked through narrow alleys, wide alleys, as he greeted some people that he passed. Ever so often he looked over his shoulder to see if I was still there, but I was slow and lagged behind. He didn't realize how painful it was for me to walk.

Finally we stopped near a run-down house with a small porch. At

Lazor's knock the door opened by a middle-aged woman wearing a white silk kerchief to cover her hair, as was the tradition for a pious woman and the wife of a rabbi.

"Good afternoon Mrs. Marcus," Lazor greeted her.

"Good afternoon," she wished him back, "What can I do for you?"

"I want to see the rabbi."

"He's taking a nap, I don't like to disturb him."

"Please, Mrs. Marcus this is an emergency, this little girl needs help for her father who was caught along with many other people by the Russian border patrol," he pleaded. She looked me over and then disappeared into another room.

I looked around the kitchen. It was neat and clean and there was the delicious smell of chicken soup and cinnamon. The table was covered with a white clean cloth and was set with a challah and polished candlesticks that had candles in them.

A short time later rabbi Marcus appeared. He was a thin man with a tattered beard and wearing a yarmulke.

"Sholom, Alehem," he greeted Lazor shaking his hand. "What can I do for you?" he asked, inspecting me.

"This little girl needs help." Lazor explained the story as best he could.

The rabbi listened attentively. After Lazor was finished the rabbi asked me, "How old are you?"

"Ten, I think."

"Mm, ten years old and you thought that you were old enough to run away. You must realize that today is Friday before the upcoming shabbos, we must wait until Sunday," he said.

I suddenly felt the tears running down my face with disappointment. "Sunday would be too late, my father and the others won't be there any more. They'll be sent away to Siberia!" I cried.

I put my head on the table cushioned by my arm and sobbed as if my heart was breaking. The Rabbi was my only hope.

Rabbi Marcus spread his hands in a helpless gesture, he didn't know what to do.

"Rabbi, it's still early," Lazor said, "may be you can make it today, it means so much to her and she's frightened."

Reb-Marcus pulled out his pocket watch, glanced at it, and then at me. He stood up looked out the window.

"Don't cry little girl I'll go and see what I can do for them."

After wishing the rabbi's wife a good shabbos, Lazor and I walked back in silence, but my heart was heavy. Suppose Papa and the others weren't there any more, I thought. Then I wondered if the rabbi knew where the Russian border was. All kinds of dreadful thoughts began to enter my mind.

Back in the store, I kept watching the clock and walking outside to see if the rabbi had freed my father.

"Malke sit down and calm yourself, give the rabbi a chance to get there," Bluma said. She brought me a glass of tea and piece of bread but I couldn't eat, I couldn't stop thinking about my father. I was sure that he was already sent to Siberia with the rest of our group.

Two hours passed and now it was sundown. I was frantic with worry. I went out and leaned against the wall of the store and peered into every face of a man with a beard hoping him to be my father.

Then my heart began to beat with excitement. My father and the others were slowly walking with the rabbi.

"Papa! Papa!" I cried and took a stumbling step forward and almost fell, but my father caught me and held me close to him.

"My God, child, where did you get the idea to run away? I ought to cut your braids off for punishment!" he said with a twinkle in his eyes and humor in his voice.

The rabbi left hastily, he was already late for the synagogue, but not before my father extended his hand to him gratefully. "I don't know how to thank you what you did for us."

"Don't thank me, thank your little girl."

The women of the group hugged me with joy. They never thought they were going to see me again, I was grateful that they didn't ask any questions. Later they parted to their own destination.

My father thanked Lazor and his wife Bluma, that wonderful couple who were so good to me. He also paid them for my food.

"I'm glad that Rabbi Marcus was able to free you all," Lazor said.

"He had to pay fifty rubles for each one of us, but thank God that we were now free to travel and continue with our journey." My father replied. "Thank you again and God bless you."

On the way to my mother, I suddenly felt the pain in my feet stronger than ever. I couldn't keep up with my father.

"Why are you limping?" he asked.

"Because my feet hurt." I replied.

I was glad that my father didn't ask me about my shoes. He stooped down and said, "get on my back I'll carry you."

Although he was tired and exhausted, my father carried me for three blocks before we got the rooming house where my mother stayed.

My fathers first words were when we entered the door, were, "Raizl, take care of Malke's feet."

My mother gasped with horror as she inspected my feet. "How in the world did you manage to walk on those blisters?" she exclaimed.

My mother didn't ask about my shoes either, but my younger brother Shloime did. "Hey, Malke, what happened to your shoes?"

I didn't answer.

"Leave your sister alone," my grandmother said.

I began to cry. "Mama, I lost my shoes."

"We'll buy you another pair," my father replied.

My mother removed my mud-splashed clothes, bathed me, put a nightie over me and doctored my feet with her homemade salve. It soon made me feel better. She wrapped my feet with white clean cloth and carried me to a cot in the bedroom. I was asleep before my mother had even left the room.

The following morning I felt refreshed and my feet felt better.

"Malke, papa says that you ran away and saved them all. But I don't understand, what made you do such a thing?" she asked, puzzled.

She couldn't understand my behavior. That a quiet child and yet do such a daring thing as to run away. "You could've gotten lost or hurt yourself real bad," my mother said with concern.

"You never know what children will do," my grandmother replied. "But thank God that everything turned out good."

It wasn't long before I began to feel like myself again. For a reward I received a new pair of shoes and a big chocolate bar, which I shared, with my brother. I also found out how my father and the rest of the group were freed from prison. The rabbi knew the headman, but that wasn't enough. Each of the families had to pay fifty rubles for their release.

I was ready to begin my new life in America.

CROSSING OVER TO AMERICA

My parents, my brother, and I stood among many other passengers who awaited the train, which would take us to Berlin. There was a young Jewish boy about sixteen who looked sad and lonely. My father, who was a friendly man, began to talk to the boy.

"I'm going to America to live with my father," the boy said. "My mother is dead."

The floor of the waiting room was littered with cigarette-buts, old papers, and dry leaves. A fringe of cobwebs was under the railway clock, which was yellowed with age and hung on the blackened wall.

It had pointed to ten o'clock for the past three hours. No one knew when the train would arrive, as there were no schedules and no timetables.

It seemed like hours and hours had passed before a train finally arrived and slowly pulled up to a stop. There was a sudden rush for the train as passengers dragged their children and bundles with unnatural energy,

My father was carrying two heavy bundles, my mother had two lighter ones, my brother held one and I carried two small bundles by strings that blistered the palms of my hands.

We ran from door to door and finally squeezed ourselves into a car. There were no benches where we could sit down so we dropped our possessions on the floor in a corner of the compartment. Then we sank down on top of our bundles, which served as our beds.

The car was overloaded with humans and bundles. The bundles were wrapped in bed sheets, boxes, sacks, and battered suitcases. A heavy smell of rotting wood and the sweat of human bodies hung in the air. The boxcar was already crowded, but more people were coming in. We hardly had an inch of space to move. It was getting stuffy and uncomfortable.

Later we munched on bread, hard-boiled eggs, and cucumbers. It seemed that everybody had become hungry because the smells of garlic, fish, chicken and other foods began to fill the cabin.

For lack of space I rested my feet on my father's lap. I looked around me and saw all the other passengers, their faces tired and pale. They, too, had the same silent look of determination as my parents. Their dreamland was "America"

Ever so often my mother looked in back of her to make sure that her best bundle was still there. Our bags and bundles which composed our traveling were much more bulky than valuable. A trifling sum of money bought steamer tickets and our passports were the magic agents from which we hoped to span the five thousand miles of earth and water between my brother Hershel and us.

How rich Hershel must be sending us all that money for our big journey all the way to America, I thought. I pictured him living in a mansion. I didn't remember my brother at all as I was still a baby when he left for the United States.

Hours passed. I heard the passengers snoring and whistling, like an orchestra. My parents and brother were sleeping, I, too was getting drowsy.

"Take your feet off my face!" I heard a woman cry out.

"Take your face away from my feet!" I heard a man's voice reply.

Later a conductor with a smoked lantern came in.

"Your documents!" he shouted to the blinking eyes of the passengers. With trembling hands my father produced the crumpled papers. After looking at them he moved to the next passenger.

After traveling all night, the train finally came to a stop early the next morning.

"Everybody out!" I heard the conductor shout. We were all glad to get out of that hot, stuffy train. The air felt good on my face, but we weren't outside for long.

The conductor hurried us into a large room. Here a great many men and women, dressed in white received us. The women attending to the women and girls while the men attended the men.

There was a scene of bewildering confusion, parents losing their children, and little ones crying. Baggage was thrown together in one corner of the yard heedless of its contents. The white clad Germans shouted commands, "Shnell! Shnell!" "Take off your clothes for the shower!"

The confused passengers obeyed all orders like meek children. I was terribly frightened, as I didn't know what to expect. I lost my mother and I felt like crying.

Everybody got undressed and we were hurried into another room where our bodies were rubbed with a slippery substance. A shower of warm water poured down on us without warning. Later we were given sheets to cover ourselves and marched to another room where the sheets were removed and a doctor looked us over to make sure that we were healthy.

"Shnell! Shnell! Get dressed or you'll miss your train!" a German yelled out.

I couldn't find my clothes, and I began to cry. I finally found my dress, but couldn't find one of my shoes. Someone had thrown it in a corner. I was nervous and upset until I found it.

Later I found my mother or rather she found me. The worst was over. Now, there was another confusion, we couldn't find our belongings among all of the bags in the pile.

Finally, we found all our bundles except one of the two goose feather pillows which my mother valued so much. She looked everywhere but it was nowhere in sight.

My mother was in tears, as we had to leave without her beloved pillows. Again we sat on the floor on our bundles. But my mother hardly said a word; she was terribly upset about the pillows.

"We'll buy new ones," my father said trying to calm her, but to no avail.

It seemed like there were constant medical examinations, which I came to dread.

"Mama, why do we have to go through so many examinations?" I asked.

"To keep us clean of diseases," she replied.

After riding in hot stuffy trains for days we finally reached Antwerp, Belgium. It was the last stop before our departure to the United States.

We were marched to a large hall where we dumped our possessions on the floor and porters put labels on them. We stayed there for a few days and were treated with food while we slept on the floors in rows. Again we had to go through another medical examination. Many passengers had been rejected for such things as hair crabs.

"Malke, my mother said, we must have a medical examination.

"What again?" I complained.

"This time is for hair lice."

"Oh, mama, I don't have any hair lice."

"Well, then there is nothing for you to worry," she replied. But I did worry. "Suppose I had some and I didn't know about it."

My heart beat with terror, as we went into the waiting room of the office where three doctors were looking over everybody's hair to make sure that there weren't any lice. Many passengers had already been rejected.

My parents, my brother, and I fearfully waited in line with beating hearts. We didn't know what to expect.

When it came to our turn, my mother walked into the office first. A few minutes later she walked out smiling, her hair was clean. Then, my father went in to see the doctor. He, too, walked out smiling. Next, my younger brother walked in for his turn, I could see that he was scared, but he went in like a little trooper. A few minutes later he came out happy. When it came to me, my heart was pounding so hard that I thought everybody could hear it. Shaking like a leaf, I slowly walked in.

"Sit down," A tall skinny doctor commanded. A nurse held up a light while he held a little comb and kept searching through my hair.

"Good," he said, "no lice."

"Mama," I screamed with excitement when I returned to the waiting room, "My hair is clean."

We all got a clean bill of health. We were one of the lucky families who were permitted to leave for the United States.

Three days later we were conducted through the gate to our ship, The Scythia, on October the ninth, 1923.

It was the first time that I had seen a large ship. Gulls flew around the ship as it slowly churned. We viewed the ship from the stone quay. The deck had been thronged by hundreds upon hundreds of foreigners, from almost every land in the world.

They came from Russia, Poland, Germany, and many others. You could tell by their native clothes the country that they had come from.

After some time, we found our way onto the ship. As the boat left the quay we looked over the railing at the land we were leaving forever.

When the shoreline finally disappeared from view we went below deck to find some room to set down our things and sleep.

When I awoke I felt sea sick and held on to the railing as I came up from below. My mother gave a piece of lemon to suck on. It made me feel better. My parents too were feeling seasick, but not my brother. It didn't seem to bother him at all. He soon found some children his age and began to play with them.

Everything was so new to me. I watched the people, the sailors, and I couldn't understand that such a large ship could stay on top of the water. Sometimes, I would watch the water from our cabin porthole, but I preferred to stay on deck and watch the ocean with the waves high as mountains. I would also see tremendous fish jump out the water really high and then fall back into the ocean.

I liked the evenings the most. After dinner there would be music and dancing. Everybody danced including the sailors and the whole kitchen staff.

One evening the band played a Polka.

"Why don't you two dance?" my mother asked my brother and I.

Without a moment hesitation, my brother and I pushed ourselves on the dance floor and began to dance the Polka.

Suddenly everybody stopped dancing and began to watch us. They clapped and whistled encouragingly. We danced fast, whirling like a spinning top. When the music finally stopped, my brother and I were out of breath.

My brother and I became celebrities overnight. After that we were made to dance every night.

We were treated with apples and sweets. People began noticing us. One

American couple tried to teach us English, and it sounded awfully hard, but I learned to count to ten in English, and a few other words.

One night a storm broke out, and the ship heaved and shuttered. Dishes broke, women screamed, children cried. I thought for sure that our ship would capsize. We weren't able sleep. I stayed close to my parents in the main room thinking the worse.

Finally after many hours the storm subsided and the ocean grew calm again. But we all had a good scare. My father didn't trust the ship but he was eventually able to fall asleep.

After being on the ship for almost two weeks I found myself counting the days when we'd get to the United States.

"Papa, how much longer will it take until we get to America?" I asked.

"Not very long, just a few more days." my father replied.

Later that week I could see the far-away lights from the cities in America. They sparkled and blinked like winking stars. Every day the cities seemed to get bigger and bigger. After the sixteen day trip, the ship finally steamed into New York Harbor and docked.

The first thing I saw was the Statue of Liberty and the American flag, which fluttered in the breeze from a high building.

Everybody was excited and kept pointing out the wonders of America to their children.

But our happiness was short lived as we were transferred to a smaller steamer and taken to a redbrick building. We entered a massive hall, which was the entire width of the building.

We were separated into dozens of lines, divided by metal railings, where we had to pass the first doctor. The men who's breathing was heavy, and women who tried to hide a limp, were marked with chalk for later inspection. Whenever a case aroused suspicion, the alien was set aside, isolated in another small room from the rest.

My parents were very fearful as we passed the doctor, who looked us over carefully, but again we passed the medical inspection without any trouble.

We were given food but we couldn't eat it because it wasn't Kosher. We lived mostly on bread and tea. We slept on wooden bunks with roll calls in the morning and night as if we were criminals.

Discomfort, hunger, humiliation were nothing to the biggest fear that was gripping us all, the chance that our family might be sent back. Many other people were isolated to be deported back to Europe.

After three weeks within the high walls and barren windows, we were finally released to my brother Hershel from the prison called, Ellis Island.

MY FIRST EXPERIENCES
IN A NEW WORLD

When my parents and I arrived to the United States, I felt as if I stepped from shadows into a bright sunlight. Almost from the first day I wanted to adopt all of the American ways, the language, ideas, clothes. I was eleven years old and soon I was going to the American school. I wanted to learn everything at once. In no time I learned to read and write.

We had only lived in our apartment for a few days when I became aware of continuous street brawls and fighting among young boys. One boy by the name of Rocky was the leader of a gang. He was a Sicilian boy of twelve, but he was tall and husky and looked almost fifteen.

One day my brother came home with a bloody nose, his hair was disheveled and his shirt was torn.

"What happened to you?" my mother asked with alarm.

"I wouldn't pay Rocky twenty-five cents a week for protection so his gang beat me up," he replied.

"What kind of protection?" I asked

"I don't know. Every new kid in the neighborhood has to pay Rocky the twenty-five cents."

"Oh, my God, what kind of a neighborhood is this? You better try to avoid them," my mother said.

"Syd, give that bully the twenty-five cents so he'd leave you alone." I suggested.

"I will not," he replied stubbornly.

We now had a problem. Syd was often threatened and was often attacked by the hoodlums, but he wouldn't give in.

One day I noticed something new in my brother's room. There was a punching bag and several pictures of professional fighters posted on the wall over his bed.

"What's all this?" I asked.

"I'm going to fight that jerk," he said while punching the bag.

"Do you really think that just by punching a bag you'll be able to fight that bully?"

"I'm taking boxing lessons."

"Boxing lessons?" I asked surprised.

"Yes."

"With whom?"

"With Maxi Fisher." he replied grinning.

I couldn't believe what I heard. "Where did you meet him? Isn't he a prize winning fighter?"

"He is my friend Al's cousin."

"So you think that you are going to become a good fighter and beat up Rocky." I said smiling.

"He's giving me lots of tips on how I can win the fight."

I didn't like the idea about my brother fighting that bully who was almost twice as big as him, but I didn't say anything. When my mother found out about what her son had in mind, she was frantic with worry.

"Sydney, give up the idea about fighting that boy. He might hurt or even cripple you and you might regret it for the rest of your life." she pleaded, but it went into deaf ears.

"Leave me alone," he yelled running into his room and punching the bag hard with all his might as if it was the bully.

After six weeks I couldn't help but notice the change in my brother.

He filled out a little and his arms became muscled. He followed Maxi's orders and it worked. My brother was now ready to fight.

One day Rocky confronted my brother.

"You want to fight me you little Jew?" he asked, cracking his knuckles.

"I'm taking boxing lessons," he told Rocky proudly. Then added, "I want it to be a real fight with boxing gloves."

"I'll fight you anyway you want."

They agreed to fight the following Sunday at two o'clock in Weehawken Park. A ring was formed from a rope on the public platform. Rocky arrived with his followers, fifteen of them! He made the sign of the cross as he entered the ring. Then he stripped off his shirt and his undershirt and began to exercise by the rope of the ring.

When Syd got into the ring, there were laughter and catcalls.

"Hey, skinny, you don't have a chance with Rocky. You better run home to your mama," one kid yelled. The crowd roared with approval.

The fight attracted many people in the park. Soon there were hundreds of spectators watching with great curiosity as the two young boys were preparing to fight. A black boy was the referee.

The bell rang and Rocky came roaring out of his corner. Sydney, too, stood up and met the bully in the center of the ring. They clinched and the referee took them apart. A moment later I thought the bully was going to knock Sydney down. But somehow my brother got away.

Later in his corner Syd got some advice from his teacher who came to see the fight. "Just give him a jab to the ribs and dance away. Don't let that bastard get in-too close. Wear him down, just keep jabbing and dancing away," Maxi told him.

Rocky was bigger and stronger than my brother, but didn't have any experience with real boxing.

"Come on, Rocky get him." they screamed. But Sydney was too fast. Rocky was now getting tired; his breathing was getting heavy and he slowing down. That's when Syd struck. He swung at the bully's head from the left and hit him right in his temple.

For a second Rocky stood there more surprised than hurt. Then he recovered and swung at Sydney like crazy, missing every time. Sydney was now jabbing with his left and got the bully on his jaw. By now the crowd had changed sides and was screaming, "Come on skinny."

The bully swung back, but missed and went down on his hands and knees. He tried to get up but fell back again.

The audience went wild as the referee raised Sydney's hand. The fight was over. Sydney had won.

IDA

Even after six weeks in America I still wore my foreign clothes. My red boots were very pretty in Poland, but not very stylish in Newark. People stared at me and at my clothes and they knew that I came from the other side. It made me feel self-conscious, but I didn't complain, as I knew my parents couldn't afford to buy me new ones.

Finally, my sister-in law felt sorry for me and bought me a new pair of shoes. I thought that the shoes were ugly. They were narrow with long pointed toes, but they were American shoes.

I couldn't help noticing how advanced my niece Ida was. She was about my age, but she was in a higher grade in school and spoke perfect English. She wasn't afraid to express her opinion about politics. Back home we had to be very careful about what we said about the government.

Ida and I got along very well. She would take me down the street to the five and ten. I would look at everything, wide-eyed with wonder. There were beads, earrings, ribbons, combs and so many other things that dazzled me.

Also, she would take me for a stroll through Prince Street where it was very crowded. I had never seen so many people in my whole life. There was a strange assortment of human beings. There were Whites, Blacks, Orientals and gypsies. On the side of the street there were pushcarts that sold bananas, a fruit that I had never seen before.

Another time Ida took me to the library. I had never seen so many books. There were tables and chairs and people sat and read or wrote something down. I always wondered how somebody had enough time to organize all of those books.

Seeing movies for the first time fascinated me. I had never seen movies before and I couldn't understand the moving figures. On the screen there was the figure of a man who was half dressed and talked with animals.

"This is Tarzan," my niece said and explained to me in Yiddish about him, and about the apes and lions that scared me, I thought for sure that they were going to jump out of the screen and attack us.

Ida and I went to the movies every Saturday afternoon. Then one day as we walked out with the crowd, I couldn't find Ida. I looked all around me, but she wasn't there. I waited outside to see if, may be she had gone to the ladies room, but the movies cleared out and new people were buying tickets.

By now I was already scared. I didn't know how to get home and I couldn't speak enough English to make a policeman understand me. I decided to look at the street signs and try to remember which way we had come from, but I couldn't remember.

It must be to the right, I thought. It was snowing and windy, but I kept on walking. I had no idea where I was going. The street was crowded with people.

I began to get uneasy. I stood there among million people, but I felt alone and helpless. I became alarmed and frightened. I started to cry. A woman stopped and asked me why I was crying, but I didn't understand her, so I walked away.

It began to get cold and I wished that I were home. I tried to walk back but I couldn't remember the street that I had come from. By now I was terrified. All of a sudden I heard a familiar voice, "Hey Molly, what are you doing here?" It was a girl Ida had introduced me to. The girl, Ana, recognized me and took me home.

When I got home there was turmoil. Ida was crying, and my brother was yelling at her, "What do you mean you leave her all alone at the movies. Go back and find her!"

I'll never forget the relief on my family's faces when they realized that I was home safe.

I forgave Ida and we became friends again, but not for long.

"You're taking all my friends away from me!" she yelled at me one day.

"How?" I asked.

"You are always telling them stories and they like to listen to you. You think that you're so pretty, but you're not!" She yelled at me

I never thought that I was pretty. Matter of fact I thought that I had an ugly nose, because my brother called me pug nose.

But despite everything I still liked her and wanted to be friends with her, even though she never forgave me.

THE RAINSTORM

Our four-room apartment on Court Street became too crowded for us. So my parents, my brother and I moved to a larger apartment on the second floor of a three-story building. Our new address was now 189 West Kinney Street.

The darkened hallway window gave us a view of the next building, which was close to ours. Going down the stairs one day something caught my eye. I paused and looked into the next apartment and my heart began racing with fear. It was a funeral parlor. I saw a coffin and a lit candle, I couldn't stand to look at it any longer and I raced up the stairs.

I was panting heavily when I entered the kitchen of our apartment. My mother looked up. "What's wrong?" she asked seeing me so out of breath.

"Mama, mama," I cried. "There are dead people in the next building!"

"You mean the funeral parlor?" she asked. "Malke, there is nothing to be afraid of, we need morticians too to bury the dead."

Leaving for school the next morning, I tried not to look through the hallway window, but just the same I was conscious of it. I ran down the stairs, open the wooden door and quickly ran out. It was the same when I came home from school.

As time passed I got used to the idea and it didn't bother me as much, until the night of a storm. The sun was still shining when my parents took my younger brother shopping while I was doing my schoolwork.

"We'll try to come home early," my mother said as she closed the door. Than added, "don't forget to do the dinner dishes."

Suddenly I heard a low rumble of thunder. I looked out the window and

I saw moving clouds slowly blocking out the sun. It looks like rain, I thought and mama didn't even take an umbrella. I decided to finish my math and then do the dishes.

It began to drizzle so I closed the windows to make sure that the rain won't come into the house. There were flashes of lightning followed by a loud roar of thunder, which made me jump. I wasn't exactly afraid, but just the same I wished that my parents were home. I filled a glass of water and put it on the windowsill just like my mother always did when there was lightning.

It's only a rainstorm, I told myself. It will pass soon. But I kept watching the time. It was still only eight o'clock and it seemed as if time didn't move. By now, the rain had really started to come down. It beat and beat against the windows, the outside walls, and the gutter.

The clap of thunder was so loud that it vibrated the whole house. It was frightening. I mustn't be afraid I told my ten-year-old mind. But just the same, it was still scary.

Suddenly the light in the kitchen went out. I tried the switches in the other rooms, but all of them were out. I looked out there were no lights anywhere in the other houses including the streetlights.

I felt my way to my room and flung myself on the bed. I huddled down in darkness and listened to the noise of the wind that moaned like a wounded dog. Lighting kept flashing jumping about the room creating weird shadows on the walls followed by the booming thunder. A window shade flew up in the kitchen and it made me hump.

I was now thinking about the funeral parlor in the next building and I shivered. I heard a door open with a creak somewhere on the upper floor. The floorboards creaked from the moving people. I clutched the pillow for support. I thought that it was a ghost.

I panicked when I heard a soft knock on the outside door of the kitchen I was too scared to go and open it. Again there was another knock on the door, harder this time.

I sat up in terror. I raised my hand to my lips to suppress a scream. Finally, I mustered up enough courage to ask who it was, "Who's there?" I asked in a weak voice.

There was nothing but silence. I couldn't move a muscle. Then I heard a woman's voice. "Let me in, it's Mrs. Greenberg, I want to borrow a candle."

What a relief I thought. I got off the bed and almost fell over a chair in my haste. "Mrs. Greenberg?" I asked to make sure.

"Yes, open the door."

I opened the door extremely fast. I was never so glad to see anybody in my whole life.

"Are you all alone?" she asked.

"Yes, my parents went shopping with my brother."

"In a night like this?"

"It was still nice when they left."

"What a storm," she remarked.

"You're lights are out too?" I asked.

"Yes, and I forgot to buy candles."

"Molly, were you afraid?"

"No," I fibbed.

"If I had known that you were all alone in the house, I would've stayed with you."

"Thanks, Mrs. Greenberg, but I wasn't afraid," I fibbed again.

"Just the same I'll stay with you until your father and mother return," she offered.

For the first time I didn't mind listening to her complaints about her arthritis and about her other problems. Time flew. The rain subsided and the lights went on again. Twenty minutes later my parents returned. Everything went back to normal again.

WORKING IN AMERICA

One day when I came home from school I saw my brother Nathan and my parents drinking tea.

"Hello Molly, we were just talking about you," Nathan said.

"Yea, about what?"

"Molly, I know what a good student you are in school, but business is bad, Papa can't get a job and…"

"You mean I have quit school?"

"There is no other way."

It was like a blow to my face. Just when I was getting ahead I was going to have to quit school. In one trimester I had already reached the sixth grade. I was dreaming about graduating and maybe going to high school.

"Mama, do I really have to leave school?"

My mother sighed. "You do need shoes, and a winter coat and some other clothes."

"Mama, couldn't I just get a job after school?"

"Maybe, but what would you do?"

"I don't know. I could baby sit."

But I couldn't get a baby-sitters job. I also tried the grocery around the corner. The owner said no before I had a chance to even finish my sentence.

"Molly," our landlady said to me one day, "Would you like to teach my three boys Yiddish. I will pay you twenty-five cents a lesson. "

"How often do you want me to teach them?" I asked,

"Three times a week," she replied.

My first teaching lesson was a disaster, they were giggling and laughing and had no respect for me as a teacher. It was no use. A week later I quit teaching and was soon recommended for a job in a factory. First I had to get working papers and I was soon made two year older. I was now fourteen years old instead of twelve.

I felt sad as I sat on the trolley car among other people who were going to work. I held on to my lunch and to the letter of recommendation to the foreman of the factory. The factory was located somewhere outside of Newark. That day it was snowing, which eventually turned into rain. My thin coat didn't keep out the cold.

I was tense as I kept looking out the window. I had no idea where the factory was. It seemed to me I was riding the trolley forever. Ever so often the trolley stopped to let in some more people. It seemed like an eternity when the conductor stopped and yelled, "Franklyn Place."

I got off the trolley and looked around. A short distance away stood a brick building of three floors crowded with windows.

Inside the smell of smoke hit my nostrils. The noise of grinding machines frightened me. I stood by the entrance watching the men work.

"Are you looking for someone," a short stocky man asked.

"Yes, I'm looking for the foreman, his name is Joe."

"I'm Joe," he said, "What can I do for you?"

I gave him my note and he read it. Ever so often he glanced at me. "You're fourteen years old?" he asked as if he didn't believe me.

I nodded.

"Come with me." he said.

I followed him up the stairs to another room. There was the noise of grinding machines coming from the where men stood and worked. There were also tables where women sat and worked on something.

I followed Joe to a table where piles of stems with green tips lay. A little flame was lit from a small pipe.

Joe picked one of the stems up and held it over the flame for a second and then put it in a long narrow wooden box. "You must be very careful not to burn the tips," he warned.

With trembling fingers I picked one of them up and held it over the flame for a second like he did.

"That's good. By the way I'll start you with seven dollars a week. Your hours are from eight o'clock till five."

I was doing all right for a few hours, but then I began to get tired.

My mind wandered back to the school that I had left and I began to burn the tips. After working for four days, I got fired.

For several weeks I couldn't get another job. One day I saw an ad in the paper from the Westinghouse looking for young girls. The ad said that no experience was necessary.

When I got there, the office was full of women and young girls. A girl gave everybody a paper to fill out. When I finished with the paper I handed it back to her.

"Sit down and wait until we call you," she told me.

After waiting for what seemed like a lifetime, my name was finally called. A nurse led me into another room where I met the doctor. He was an elderly man with white hair and a stethoscope, which was stuck in his ears. The nurse helped me to a long table and told me to lie down. The doctor listened to my heart, and looked into my mouth. He had me cough several times and then began to ask me questions.

"Do you sweat at night when you sleep?"

"Sometimes." I said as I thought of the hot summer days.

"Do you feel tired?"

"Sometimes," I replied.

"How is your appetite?"

"Okay I guess, but most of the time I'm not hungry."

The doctor kept asking me all kinds of questions, and I thought I gave him normal answers.

He began looking at me strangely. He wrote something down on a pink slip and told me to hand it to the girl in the office.

When I gave the slip to the red-haired girl, she too, looked at me strangely. "Try to get well first honey, before you look for a job."

"What do you mean?"

"You didn't get the job because you're sick."

"What 's wrong with me?" I asked.

"You have a bad heart," she replied solemnly.

I was stunned. I was never seriously sick beside a cold. People with bad hearts usually die. I wondered how long I had left to live.

When I got home I could hardly talk. I walked into my room and lay down on the bed.

"What's wrong, didn't you get the job?" my mother asked.

"No, Mama."

"Why not? "

"Because the doctor told me that I have a bad heart. Mama, I'm a very sick girl."

"Nonsense. Come on I'll take you to Dr. Waters."

After we arrived at his office I told Dr. Waters what the doctor at the Westinghouse office had told me. He gave me a careful examination.

When he was finished he said, "I wish I were as healthy as you are." He wrote something down on a piece of paper and said, "Take this to the factory."

This time, when I went to the Westinghouse factory, they hired me. After working there for only a short time I began to find the job monotonous. I felt terribly confined. After two weeks I quit.

I was restless and unhappy. I still missed school. I wished my father could find a job. I envied one of my friends. Ann's father was a shoemaker, he was making a living so his daughter could go to school.

I couldn't stand being confined in factories so I decided to find a selling job. I tried the Woolworth store, and then Bamberger's department store, but they wouldn't hire anybody without a diploma from school. I felt like a burden to my parents and my brothers.

One day I saw an ad in the paper. It sounded very attractive. It said that experience was not necessary, and that I could make from twenty to thirty dollars a week by selling items to housewives. I liked the idea of selling so I decided to walk down there. It was only a few blocks from where I lived.

The place looked like a drugstore packed with merchandise. There were many people ahead of me. Nobody paid any attention to me as I stood in line with the rest of the people. I stood there listening to a man wearing a white jacket. He was explaining to everybody about the job. "You can make yourself a few nice dollars just by selling these easy items to housewives. A housewife could always use laundry soap," the owner explained, "They need toothpaste, face powder, cold cream, lipstick, aspirins, peroxide, and mercury chrome. All these things are the basics and are easy to sell."

I felt excited with the prospect of selling. I'll be my own boss, I thought.

When Mr. Smith was through talking, everybody pushed forward. Mr. Smith wrote down everybody's name and address, counted the items as he put them into a satchel and wished them luck. When it finally came my turn Mr. Smith smiled but didn't ask my age, which I was grateful for. He brought out a small satchel, counted off ten items, placed them in the satchel and handed it to me. He also handed me a small memo pad and a pencil to marked down orders for items I didn't have.

Outside, I didn't know where to turn. I didn't know the neighborhood, but I decided to try one of the houses anyway. I rang the bell, but no one answered, so I tried the door and I saw a woman doing something.

"How dare you open the door!" she shouted.

"I'm sorry I thought I heard, somebody say 'come in'."

"I said no such thing!" she screamed, "Get the hell out!" I scurried out so fast I almost fell over my valise.

My heart was pounding with the insult. I never expected anything like that. I was afraid to go to the next house so I decided to go to the neighborhood where I lived.

I braved myself as I knocked on a door. No one answered, but I didn't dare to try to open it again. So I went to the next house and tried again. This time a black woman opened the door and invited me inside. I noticed she was washing clothes.

After I showed he my items she said, "I can use some soap. How much is it?"

"Five cents a piece," I said, barely able to keep the excitement of my first sale out of my voice.

"All right, give me three pieces."

With trembling fingers I took out the three pieces of soap and handed them to her. She paid me fifteen cents.

"Would you like some face powder or lipstick?" I asked.

"No, dear, I never use that stuff."

I marked down the sale in my pad. I was never so happy. I decided to go onto Broome Street where all of the black people lived. I was surprised to find them friendly. Some bought the items that I had and some gave me orders for certain items that I didn't. When I got home I counted my items and money. I sold almost three dollars worth. I made thirty cents for a few hours work.

The following day I set out at nine o'clock in the morning. This time I tried an apartment building. I tried two flights of doors and hardly sold anything, but I didn't get discouraged I just moved on and kept trying. At the end of the week, I sold five dollars worth of items and a few orders for items that I didn't have with me.

I went back to Mr. Smith for the items people ordered and he was very pleased. I had made ninety cents in my first week. "I'm sure you'll do better next week," Mr. Smith said encouragingly.

The following Monday I decided to try and sell to a different neighborhood where mostly Polish people lived. They admired the articles, but didn't buy anything. Again I climbed stairs, sometimes up to the third floor, but I sold very little. Sometimes they wouldn't even open up their door, but I still wasn't discouraged. I kept climbing stairs and knocking on doors. Then one day a woman opened the door and invited me in.

"What do you have to sell?" she asked.

I opened the satchels and was about to take out an item when I cut my finger in the piece of tin that was near the opening of the case. My finger started to bleed.

"Go to the sink and wash the blood off," she said.

I went into the kitchen and washed off my finger, which was bleeding pretty badly.

I put a handkerchief around my finger, but it still hurt. When I came back the lady was looking at my articles and then told me that she couldn't use any of them. I felt disappointed and left.

When I came home and counted the articles, I noticed a jar of cold cream was missing and a lipstick. My heart fell. It never dawned on me that people could be dishonest. After trying a few more times I decided to give that selling job up. After paying out of my own pocket for the items that I had lost, I came out with fifty cents for the whole week. For the two weeks I was working I only made one dollar and forty cents.

Again I was without a job. But I wouldn't work in a factory any more. I only wanted to sell, but no one wanted to hire me. I was too young and inexperienced.

One day I passed a hat store. On the window was a sign that said that an experienced saleslady was needed. I read the sign, but I didn't think that the owned would hire me. I walked back and forth several times and after much thought, I finally walked inside the store. There were racks and racks of all different kinds of hats. There were large brims, small brims, straw hats, silk ones, and a great variety of ladies hats.

"What can I do for you?" a stout lady asked.

"Are you the owner of the store?" I questioned.

"Yes."

"I noticed that you're looking for a saleslady."

"Are you experienced?"

"I didn't sell any hats, but I sold other things."

She looked me over. "I pay eight dollars a week, if you are good, I'll give you a raise.

"You mean you're hiring me?" I asked, my heart pounding with excitement. I couldn't believe my own ears.

"You will have to work from nine to six on Monday to Thursday and until ten at night on Friday and Saturday. My name is Mrs. Piddle."

I went home happy for the first time. Even if she had only offered me five dollars a week, I would've taken the job.

I found that the job was just what I wanted to do. I treated the black people with silk gloves and made them feel important. They began asking for me whenever they came in. In a short amount of time, I topped the other two salesgirls. I loved the job and I loved Mrs. Piddle. After two months she gave me a raise of a dollar. I was now making nine dollars a week and I felt rich. I gave my mother five dollars and kept four.

In the slow season she let the other two girls go and kept me on. She began to trust me with signing for the merchandize when it came in. Sometimes I would suggest to her how to arrange some of the hats. She began to depend on me and it made me feel good. The salesmen would talk to me, but I would blush and turn away. I remember one of the salesmen tried to make a date with me, but I refused. I was too shy.

One day, as I walked home, I ran into one of the girls I had gone to school with.

"Hi Molly," she said cheerfully.

"Hi Ann," I replied.

"Are you working?"

"Yes, in Mrs. Piddle's hat store. How are you doing in school?" I asked.

"I skipped the eighth grade and I expect to graduate at the end of the semester. It's a shame that you had to drop out of school. You were the best in our class."

"I had to, I wish that I could have stayed," I said.

All of the old hurts about school began to stir up so I quickly excused myself and left. I wished that my father was a tradesman, like Ann's, instead of a scholar.

When I entered the kitchen, my mother was surrounded by pots and pans, as usual. I sniffed in the direction of the stove. Whatever she was making smelled delicious. I sat down at the table and my mother put a bowl of soup in front of me. Remembering my conversation with Ann, I suddenly lost my appetite.

"Why aren't you eating your soup? It will get cold," my mother scolded.

"I'm not hungry," I replied.

"Is anything wrong?" she asked.

I burst into tears and told her about Ann

"Mama, I wanted to graduate so much, and now I will never get to."

"You must never give up hope. You'll catch up some day, you'll see," she replied optimistically.

In the next couple of weeks things began to look up. Mrs. Piddle gave me several more raises and I was now making twelve dollars a week. I opened up a bank account and I tried to save two to three dollars a week. I gave my mother five dollars but I also bought things for the house or for my mother that I knew she needed. So I really didn't have much left. I loved my job and my boss who was very good to me. The hat store was like a school to me as I met so many people and I loved to wait on them. All in all I was quite content.

NATHAN'S STORE

I had worked at the hat store for over a year when my older brother, Nathan, came over to the house one evening and asked me if I would like to work for him. "Molly, I'll pay you exactly what Mrs. Piddle pays you," he promised. Suddenly, my heart became heavy. I didn't want to leave my job with Mrs. Piddle.

"I'm sorry Nathan, I couldn't possibly leave my job," I replied.

"Why not?" my brother wanted to know.

"Because my boss needs and depends on me."

"I need you too, there is no one that I can trust to run my ladies' wear store," he said.

"What about Jenny?" I asked.

"Molly, my wife has three children to take care of, besides she's doing the sewing on the new aprons for the store. You see, I have to go to New York to buy new things for the store and I can't possibly close down the store for that long of a time. I would lose too much business," he replied.

"Let me think about it Nathan", I said.

That night I could hardly sleep. I was so use to listening to my elders that it was very hard for me to say no to my brother. So I tried to avoid him as much as possible.

One afternoon my brother came into the hat store without greeting me. He walked over to Mrs. Piddle and spoke to her in low tone of voice. I could see that Mrs. Piddle became upset. She kept looking at me as if she was trying to read my mind. My heart was so heavy that I avoided her eyes.

After talking to him, she came over to me. "I'll give you another raise," she said. She thought that it was just an excuse that my brother was there. She thought that I wanted more money.

"Mrs. Piddle, my brother opened up a lady store and he has no one to help him," I explained.

But Mrs. Piddle was still upset and angry when I left. I too was upset and angry with my brother who took me away from a job that I liked so much.

Nathan's store of was located on Prince Street, one of most hectic and busiest areas in Newark. Stores stood close to each other, selling all kinds of merchandise. There was tremendous competition between merchants for business.

The street was always crowded with an assortment of human beings. There were whites, blacks, gypsies, thieves, and even gangsters. The activity of business went on until late at night. There were the pushcarts on the side of the street laden with all kinds of fruit and vegetables and even clothing for a bargain price.

My brother's store stood among many others. With a big sign on the window that read "Nathan Sherman's Bargain Store."

It was right across the street from my brother Hershel's Hardware store. I could see that Hershel wasn't too pleased as Nathan also carried yard goods among his ready-made merchandise.

The store itself wasn't big at all. It was dark, damp with a foul smell of fish, which came from the fish store next door. The shelves on one side of the wall were packed with boxes of ladies and children's socks, stockings, braziers and underwear. On the other side of the wall was a rack where ladies cheap housedresses, and robes were hanging. A housedress was displayed on the outside door with a special price as an advertisement. On the wall was a long string from one end to another with extra sizes of ladies panties.

There was no dressing room except in the back of a fixture in the back of the store. It was more like a corner with a curtain for privacy. The fixture was specially made with drawers for underwear. What my brother failed to realize was that there was no back on the drawers so they could also be opened from the back.

The window was a fairly good size and dressed with all kinds of merchandize including dresses, robes, aprons, sweaters, underwear and many other items.

"Nathan, how am I supposed to be able to remember all those things? It really scares me to handle so many items and have to remember all of those prices."

"I'll stay with you for the whole week and mark down the prices for you," he replied.

I'll never forget the first day that I was left alone in the store. I was scared stiff. I looked inside the boxes and tried to remember where everything was. A small black woman came into the store and asked for a large size of underwear. As I turned my back to look for her size she grabbed the large sizes from the string that Nathan displayed over the counter and quickly ran out the store.

I was afraid to tell my brother, so to cover it up; I displayed another pair of large panties on the string. Every time a customer walked into the store I had to watch them, but they were more experienced than me. I was young and they found many good opportunities to steal. They found ways to steal so that I didn't even realize that anything was gone until they had already left the store.

One day three gypsies walked into the store and asked for a dress in the window. I got them the dress and tried to watch them in the same time. They took the dress to the back of the store to try it on. They were there a long time and were talking in a language I didn't understand.

They finally came out gave me back my dress and told me that it didn't fit and walked out.

Later, when I opened one of the drawers from the big fixture for underwear, when a customer asked, it was completely empty. I was flabbergasted. I was sure that my brother filled it up with all kinds of underwear. It was not until later that I realized that they had taken the items from the back of the fixture.

It seemed that every crook knew by now that a young girl was left alone in a certain store and they all came to rob and steal.

One day my brother said, "Molly, I don't understand there is hardly any money in the register and lots of merchandise is missing." He said it in such a tone as if he thought that I was the thief. I felt hurt and insulted.

I was so young and inexperienced. Why couldn't my brother understand that? I bit my lip and didn't answer. I still had no choice but to work for him. Once he caught me reading a magazine and he became very angry.

"Is that all you got to do is read when there is so much work to do?" he yelled at me. I felt guilty and put the magazine away. There was no end to the work that I had to do. It was always so dusty and once I saw a rat in a corner it almost as big as a cat. I was so frightened that I ran outside.

One late afternoon, towards evening, a man came in. He was shabby looking and I didn't like it.

"What can I do for you?" I asked, but he didn't answer. I didn't like his shifty eyes. My heart began to pound with fright, as I was alone in the store. I felt trapped alone with a man who looked like a gangster. Suddenly, I got an idea.

"Do you want to see my brother?" He didn't answer but took a step towards me. I moved away. "I'll call him out, he's in the washroom."

I stuck my head behind the curtain of the dressing room and began to call my brother. "Nathan, there is some one here who wants to see you," I whispered, so the man would think that I spoke to someone. To my surprise the man turned and walked out. My heart was still pounding with fright when Nathan came in a half hour later.

"You did the wise thing," he said with concern. "I'll try to come in earlier next time."

After working for another few weeks I felt that I couldn't cope with the thieves and I had no idea how to run his business so I quit.

I couldn't go back to my old boss because I knew how upset she was when I left, besides she hired someone else to replace me.

Again I was out of a job. I was very resentful towards my brother for taking me away from a job that I really enjoyed.

The only thing for me to do was to try other stores where they might hire me. But they all had the same answer. "I'll let you know." It was impossible for me to get a job.

One day a girl I knew, Helen, told me that she worked in a factory, sewing bands on men's hats. "The girls are making good money and so do I," she said. "They're not hiring anybody right now, but they might hire you on my recommendation."

"But I don't know nothing about sewing and besides, I'm left-handed," I countered.

"It doesn't matter, you'll learn," Helen said.

So the next morning 1 went along with Helen to the factory where she worked, all the way in Clifton, New Jersey. The factory was a two-story brick building. When we entered the factory, Helen introduced me to the forelady, Mrs. Brown. She looked me over thought for a moment. "Do you have any experience in this line of work?" she asked.

"No, ma'am, this is my first time," I replied.

"All right, I'll show you how it's done," she said.

I followed her to one of the tables that other girls were working on and told me to sit down. I watched the girls working on the men's hats, their needles and thread flying back and forth on the band of the hat. Mrs. Brown gave me a carton of twelve hats and showed me what I had to do. "I pay ten cents a hat", she said. "The girls are doing about two cartons a day sometimes more, it's all up to the worker. It depends how fast you are."

I felt terribly clumsy as I tried to do one in front of the forelady. "Don't worry, you'll get the hang of it," she encouraged and left.

I watched the girls who were sewing with remarkable speed. By the time I finished one they were on their sixth. I pricked my finger and it bled. At the end of the day my fingers were so sore that I could hardly bend them or straighten them out. Sometimes the felt of the hat would be extra tough and the needle won't go through, it would slip and prick my finger, but I would ignore it and keep on working.

No matter how fast I tried to be, when the day ended I had only made seven or eight hats. "You'll do better as you keep practicing," my friend said, "give it a chance."

I had no choice, as there were no other jobs available. After working a week I began to make a little more money but I never made more than seven dollars a week. The work was hard and I was miserable.

One day I worked extra hard and my fingers were sore from the hats that were extra tough. The needle just wouldn't go through the cloth. I was glad when the day was over. I was about to take my tickets from under the brown paper where I put them, when I saw that they weren't there.

Each ticket meant ten cents. I had seven tickets for a whole days work.

Somebody had taken them when I left to go to the washroom. The forelady was sympathetic but couldn't do anything for me. "You have to watch your tickets," she said, "it happens quite often."

That week ended up with less than six dollars that week so I quit.

Again I was out of a job. I wanted so much to go back to the hat store that I was working at before my brother Nathan took me away to work with him, but I didn't have the nerve to face her.

The next week my old boss somehow spotted me and called me in. I was never so glad to see anybody in my whole life. I told her everything that had happened since I left her store. She understood my situation better after I explained about my brother and how miserable I was leaving her.

"Molly, would you like to come back to work for me?" Mrs. Piddle asked, then she added, "You know, quiet a few customers still ask about you."

"I'd love to. Thank you so much Mrs. Piddle," I said as my heart filled with joy.

The next day I walked excitedly into the hat store and met the new employee that she had hired in my absence. I became good friends with the girl named Judy, who was very nice to me.

BEAUTY CONTEST

"Molly, would you like to go to a beauty contest?" Judy asked me one day.

"Sure I would love to. I've never seen one before.

"It's going to be in Kruger's Auditorium next Sunday night."

That evening, looking at my clothes closet, I couldn't find anything decent to wear.

The stores on Springfield Avenue were open on Sunday, so I hurried Sunday morning to look for a new dress. Some of the dresses were too fancy and too expensive. But I spotted a blue cotton polka-dress

"It's the only one I have left," the owner told me, "what size do you wear?"

"I don't know."

"Try it on, it looks like it will fit you."

The dress fit me like a glove. I liked the high mandarin collar with the full skirt. The price was five dollars. It was such a good deal that I bought it.

When I arrived at the ballroom, it was ablaze with light. The orchestra was playing and couples were dancing on the high polished floor. I noticed young girls were wearing silk dresses, high-heeled shoes, earrings, and necklaces, their hair was combed beautifully. I suddenly felt out of place with my cotton dress. I hid myself in a corner sat on a bench and watched them dancing. Judy was also dressed in a nice silk dress. She sat with me at first, but then she saw some friends and walked away. A blond-haired boy came over and asked me for a dance. I said no because I was too embarrassed to be seen with my polka dress.

Finally, I saw a tall man appear on the stage talking on the microphone, announcing that the beauty contest was about to begin. Everybody moved forward to have a better look on the girls who formed a single line dressed in their beautiful gowns. I thought they were all beautiful. There were three men sitting on the stage as judges. The orchestra began to play as the girls walked around the stage.

Everybody applauded, and some men whistled. Little by little girls were eliminated until there were only three of them left. The tall blond girl won third price, then the shorter girl with the curly hair won second prize and the girl with the blue gown and blue eyes won first prize.

People were clapping and whistling and making a lot of commotion. Everybody was excited and talked amongst themselves after the contest was over.

"Ladies and Gentlemen," the same man on the microphone said. "Your attention, please." Again, everybody moved forward to hear what he had to say. "The Judges and I have spotted a young lady on the floor who we think deserve a prize."

Everybody looked at each other wondering who the lucky young lady is, including me. It must be the girl with the pink dress, I thought, I admired her all night. I thought that she was awfully pretty.

"You, young lady, come up the stage," he said, pointing my way. "You, young lady with the blue polka dress."

I was frozen to the floor. He couldn't mean me with my cheep little dress, but he did. I slowly moved toward the stage.

He put his arm around me. "Ladies and Gentlemen, don't you think that she is pretty?"

I felt my cheeks get red. "What's your name?" he asked me.

"Molly Sherman." I blurted out.

By now everybody was clapping and whistling. I felt terribly embarrassed The M.C. finally gave me a white envelope. "Did anybody ever tell you how pretty you are?" he asked.

"No," I murmured as I walked down the stairs from the stage and back among the audience, I suddenly became a celebrity. Girls walked over and asked me all kinds of questions.

"What kind of rouge do you use?"

"I don't use any."

"Come on, I don't believe you."

She took out a handkerchief, wet it with water and rubbed one of my cheeks, but I got redder instead. There was nothing on the handkerchief. She was amazed.

When I got home I opened my gift. There was a ten-dollar bill. I had a lot of plans for that money. I needed shoes and a blouse.

Suddenly I thought of my mother, I went out and walked into a jewelry store. I bought her a golden wedding band, which she needed badly. Her silver ring was already black with age.

The ring cost seven dollars. I had it wrapped in a nice little box and held it tight as I walked home.

"Mama, I got something for you," I said when I walked in the house

She was baking something in the kitchen, her hands full of flour. "For me?" she asked.

"Yes mama, for you," I replied. I'll never forget the look on her face when she saw the ring.

"Malke, is this gold?"

"Yes mama, it is."

She slipped off her old blackened ring and tried the new one on. It fit her finger perfectly. My mother kept looking at it as if she never saw anything like it before.

"It's unbelievable, I can't believe how beautiful it is."

I was so happy that my mother liked the ring. It never even occurred to me that I could have spent the money on myself.

MY FIRST ROMANCE

One day my brother Sydney brought home a new friend and introduced me to him. "Molly, meet Sam Crawitz. He' s in my music class, he plays the violin."

"Oh, how nice," I replied shyly.

"Nice to meet you," Sam said, "Sydney told me all about you."

"I hope it was all good things."

"He told me that you were very pretty, and he was right."

"Thank you," I replied, blushing. I was only fifteen and was still very shy with boys.

Sam wasn't too good looking, but he looked older than seventeen, but his voice was soft and gentle as he spoke. Later he played his violin for me and I was very impressed. It was a song from Mozart.

It was love at first sight on my part and I was hoping that he would like me too. Eventually he asked me too a movie and I agreed.

We went to see a Charlie Chaplin movie. I felt excited as he took my hand and held it firmly. I heard the people in the movie laughing as Chaplin performed, but I didn't see or hear a thing. As for Sam, his eyes never left me.

Sometimes Sam would take me to a free concert or for a walk in the park. He would often talk to me about his dreams and music. I pictured him playing in Carnegie Hall some day and that people would stand in line for hours and pay all kinds of money to hear him play.

On one of the walks in the park, Sam looked in my eyes as if trying to read my mind of some nameless secret. "You are so sweet," he murmured in my ear. "I love you," he whispered, "Will you marry me some day?"

"I love you, too," I replied.

"We'll have a big house, a car, and jewelry, everything your heart desires," he promised.

The next day, the iceman brought up the ice and arranged it in our icebox, my father greeted him with a good morning. Although my father had been a studious man he was friendly to every human being he met.

"It's hard work what you do, carrying all that ice on your back and climbing so many stairs."

The iceman was glad to unburden himself and poured out his heat to my father's sympathetic ear. "I have a son, but he's too lazy to help me. All he wants to do is playing the violin. He'll never amount to anything.

"One of my son's friends plays a violin," my mother asked.

"Is your son's name Sydney?"

"Yes, how did you know?"

"Both my son and yours play in the music class at school."

"How old is your son?" My father asked.

"He'll be eighteen in June."

"He should be working." my mother remarked.

"He works in a gas station a few days a week, but that is no help to me." The iceman complained.

When Sam's father said this, I dropped my spoon into the cereal I was eating. Sam was the son of this shabby iceman? Papa would die if he knew that I was going steady with him. I recalled the way that he demolished my older sisters dates.

He did little things like quizzing them about their families, background, and their trades. If their fathers were tailors, carpenters, or any other type of tradesman, he end of their date. None of the men my sisters picked were good enough to be accepted into our family. My two older sisters lost many good chances at marriage. They finally left for Chicago to visit my brother. There they found men on their own and got married. Unfortunately their marriages didn't turn out well.

I still went out with Sammy. I loved him for him and I didn't care what his father was doing for a living. I'm no going to tell papa about us, I thought. I'll keep it a secret for a while.

"Malke, is it true that you are going out with the iceman's son?" My father asked me one day.

"Yes, papa, it's true." I blurted out.

"You will never see that boy again!" he told me sternly.

"But papa, he's a nice boy, and I love him."

"Stop that nonsense! You're not allowed to see that boy again."

"Papa, this is America not Russia!" I countered. "You're old fashioned, young girls chose their own husbands here."

"But family and background is very, very important," my mother said.

"Sam is a nice boy. I can't see why he should be blamed because his father is an iceman. Besides," I added, "it's not like he's a criminal, he makes an honest living."

But my father won. I eventually gave up Sammy, my romance ended. Although it took me a long time to get over it.

EPILOGUE

'My First Romance" was the last story that Molly wrote. After this she went on to lead a very fulfilling life in America. She got married to Edwin Pollack, had four kids, Robert, Elizabeth, Marilyn, and Eleanor, and eventually opened her own business on Staten Island. After her kids were married, Molly and Edwin moved to Florida where she lived out the rest of her days until she past away on December 19, 1982.

www.ingramcontent.com/pod-product-compliance
Lightning Source LLC
Chambersburg PA
CBHW030412290526
45785CB00004B/1979